A Few Words About, "The "Norm

This book has its foundation laid articles I have written about my family and my role in it. I am not shy about sharing my story. In fact, it is a common topic I bring up with the people who have the patience to listen to me.

However, there was great hesitation on my part in writing this book. I am sadly lacking in technological skills. Previously, when I self-published booklets, I had either my daughter, Robin Nankin, or my best friend, Rose Vieira, to do all the required groundwork for me. Later, my friend, Andrea Bolender, obtained professional help to make my last booklet a reality.

But now I found another assistant to help me. His name is Scott Nankin, and he is not only my grandson, he is a computer whiz.

Yet, even with Scott's offer to help, and Andrea sending me a new computer to contribute to this project, I still hesitated. I fear failure. Not that I haven't known failure before, because I have. But this kind of failure is about not doing justice to my family's memory. Will what I tell you make you remember them? Or will what I say fall short?

Today is October 29. It is my brother, Russell's birthday. But he is celebrating it in heaven with the rest of my family. He has been dead since 1982. He was 23.

He, unlike me, was a positive person. He saw good in people, and he brought out the best in them. He thought he could beat Duchenne Muscular Dystrophy, that there would be a cure for both him and our younger brother, Stuie. He lived his life believing he had a future, so the time he was alive, brief as it was, he had a full life. Russell met Jerry Lewis in person. He explored the Carribean with our Mom's help. He was Bar Mitzvah. And best of all, he was the sports announcer for the Rhode Island College Girls' Basketball Team.

I keep thinking of how he is looking down at me and willing me to believe in myself enough to write this book. He wants me to do this, not for fame or fortune, but to feel a sense of accomplishment and worth I have always lacked.

It was Russell who convinced Daddy to keep believing in me as I made a mess of my life. I married a bad man after our little brother passed away. He encouraged Daddy to continue to pay my college tuition. He asked Mom to do what she could for me.

As Russell laid brain dead, with wires invading his body, his spirit beckoned to me to ask our parents to free him from his body, to let his soul ascend to heaven.

I did, and they listened to me.

Russell had helped me in my life, at a time before I realized he had. It took me years to understand the relationship I had with Russell. I was much closer to my younger brother, Stuie. But Russell still fulfilled his role as my older brother, despite his physical decline from Muscular Dystrophy.

And so, in honor of what would have been Russell's 59th birthday, I decided that I am going to write this book.

I hope the journey you are about to take with me will be meaningful for both of us.

I lovingly dedicate this book in memory of my parents, David and Tina Chernick, and to my late siblings, Russell, Stuart, and Anita Chernick.

May their memory continue to be a blessing to me.

Chapter 1:

Before the Birth of   "The "Normal "Child".

Before the birth of "The "Normal Child", my Mom had three pregnancies. Her first pregnancy came six weeks after her marriage to my father. Tina and David met on a blind date Mrs. Lowry set up. They courted very briefly, going to Roger Williams Park, when Daddy wasted no time in proposing.

David Chernick was 37 at the time. He had been a chubby child, learning to play piano instead of playing sports. He had two friends slip through the ice as he struggled to put his ice skates on. He never got beyond feeling guilty that he had survived because he had been too fat to get his skates on sooner.

Daddy had dreamt of going to law school. Instead, his father forced him to become a bail bondsman, to make it a family business. He lived with his parents as his younger sisters married. He seemed to live in the shadows of his father's demands.

Then World War 2 began for America, after the bombing of Pearl Harbor. Daddy was drafted into the army. But he went willingly to serve his country. His troop landed in Marseilles, and they made their way up to Alsace-Lorraine, into Germany.

There, in the outskirts of Munich, they discovered Dachau. What Daddy saw there never left him alone for the rest of his life.

David Chernick came home in 1946. He returned to his routine of bailing people out of jail and living with his parents. But by 1949, he knew, at age 37, that it was now or never to have a life of his own.

He met Tina Korner. She was originally from Vienna, Austria. A gifted student, she dreamt of becoming a medical doctor. Her father, especially, supported his youngest daughter's goal.

Tina was the youngest of 6 children. The eldest daughter ended up in the Steinhof, due to being compromised, and died there under mysterious circumstances. A son died in the Lainz Neuromuscular Hospital. Another brother played chess and soccer, with no disability whatsoever. A sister was a beauty and daredevil, another sister was a dutiful daughter.

Tina was beyond bright. She was brilliant as well as hardworking. She put in the time to achieve the top grades and scores on report cards and exams for continuing high level studies.

But Hitler happened. He brought Nazi rule with the annexation of Austria. The Viennese Jewish girl's dreams were smashed to pieces. Her brother ended up in both Dachau and Buchenwald, before being released, and then fled before the start of World War 2.

The rest of them went to Italy, first free, then interned, hunted down, hidden, briefly freed, only to be interned in the one refugee camp in the United States.

When they were truly allowed to stay, they came to Providence, Rhode Island.

3 years later, on November 24, 1949, Tina Korner married David Chernick at Beth Shalom Synagogue.

But Mom wore a suit. At age 28, in those days, was not considered a young bride. The groom, now 38, was thought to be nearly beyond marriage.

Their union was not a big affair. The reception was a Thanksgiving meal at the groom's parents' home. There was a cake, but it was a birthday cake for a 2 year old niece.

The honeymoon was a weekend in New York. They took the train from Union Station in Providence. When they returned, David bought a tenement. The couple lived downstairs while a tenant occupied the top floor.

It was located on West Clifford Street in South Providence, a neighborhood to later to be in decline.

It was here where Tina got pregnant after 6 weeks of marriage. But all was not well. Tina had trouble gaining weight. It had been 4 plus years since her ordeal ended.

Yet, she hardly looked pregnant. Her doctor worried what the result would be.

Anita Chernick was born weighting just more than 5 pounds. It was feared something would be wrong. Mom refused to accept anything was amiss. But Daddy saw Anita not meeting milestones. The doctor agreed.

Anita attended Hebrew Day School, but the principal insisted that Anita be tested by a psychologist. The results were upsetting. Anita had an IQ of 74. It was borderline retarded. She could be trained for some lower level job. Mom couldn't accept this evaluation. She had been through so much already in her life. But Daddy understood that Anita needed to go to a public school where she could learn on her own level.

At Flynn, Anita made a friend named Nancy. She was Chinese, had a large family, and patience for my sister. Anita was welcomed into their home to play. No one made fun of her . She was treated kindly. Anita felt like she belonged.

Because in school, Anita couldn't keep up. There was no special education available then. So Anita had to repeat a grade. But she did learn very basic reading and math skills. She made some progress.

Meanwhile, in 1954, Hurricane Carol came roaring into Providence. There was little advance warning back then. Daddy was missing. Mom had been pregnant. But the weather caused dogs to be confused. One dog tried to attack Anita. Mom shielded her daughter from harm, but then began to bleed badly. She was rushed to the hospital, but it became a serious miscarriage.

Daddy had taken refuge in a tall building downtown. He was found and had to go to the hospital to comfort his wife. Anita was to be their only child, so said the doctors.

David began to make a better living so he sent Tina and Anita to a summer cottage to escape the heat. He let Tina buy pretty dresses. And he tried to help when Anita experienced temper tantrums. He would take her for drives late at night.

Then Tina's sister died suddenly. Regina Korner had a ruptured appendix. Not only had she been the dutiful daughter, but the faithful sister and helping aunt.

Mom was heartbroken over yet another loss.

But some years ago, her brother had been located living in Israel. Abe came to America in 1951, to help with aging parents, and a sister who had becoming mentally ill.

From grief came an unexpected development. Tina was pregnant again! It was a miracle, or so it seemed. This pregnancy was a healthy one. Mom gained the desired weight. And a big, baby boy was born. They named him Russell, after Regina.

Mom was so proud of her son. Daddy was thrilled at age 47 to finally have a son. Russell was meeting his milestones with everything. There was no reason at all to worry.

Then came another pregnancy just 9 months later.

David was making a good living by this time. His dream was

to move to the suburbs, to have a big yard for the children, and more bedrooms. This was to be a third child.

So with Tina 8 months pregnant, David bought with cash on the house at 46 Eldridge Street in Cranston.

Anita got her own big bedroom. Her paternal grandparents bought her a bedroom set.

Russell had his own medium sized room.

And the baby would have a smaller room for a bedroom.

But for Anita, this move was not wanted. Her friend, Nancy, remained in the deteriorating neighborhood. Worst of all, Anita had to repeat a grade again. She did not meet the standard for entering 4th grade for Cranston Public Schools. Anita was a chubby girl, she could not pass for younger. She was obviously two years older than those in third grade.

In her eyes, she saw the new baby as responsible for all her hardships. A baby girl was born in June of 1960.

She seemed normal in every way. Her parents welcomed her, calling her Cynthia. But Daddy decided the nickname Cindy suited me better.

Chapter 2: The Early Years

Thus, began my life. The day I came home from the hospital, Daddy walked to the store to buy me baby formula. As he crossed Pontiac Avenue, he was hit by a truck. He was rushed to a different hospital.

My earliest memories of Daddy is him wearing that neck brace. He had to wear it for the first five years of my life.

But I think how fortunate I was that Daddy survived what happened to him that day. How different my life would have been without him in it.

Because he survived that day, I had a baby brother born in February of 1963. Unlike how Anita felt about my birth, I was delighted the day Stuart Scott Chernick was brought home from the hospital.

Stuie, seemingly, was the healthy baby boy tipping the scale at 8 pounds, 13 ounces. For the first two years of his life, he reached all his milestones. And his temperament was wonderful.

I remember asking Daddy to lift me into his crib so I could play with him. My request was granted. Honestly, I can say I loved Stuie from the very beginning. We were inseparable early on.

As Stuie left babyhood into young childhood, we developed playing with both matchbox cars and Dawn Dolls. We created our pretend family. We used both the den table and Daddy desk with a roll out feature that bridged both pieces of furniture so we had more space.

After we were done playing, we put all our toys away in the toy box Daddy bought for us, knowing we needed a safe place for our beloved dolls and play cars, as well as small furniture we used in our make believe house.

The den also was Daddy's makeshift office. There was a phone in there for Mom to answer, "Mr. Chernick's office", if Daddy wasn't home.

As I got older, I sometimes had to answer that phone as well, to take messages, or to find out who it was, so Daddy could decide whether to take the call or not.

It was odd to me that Anita was never allowed to answer Daddy's business phone. The boys never did either.

At first, it was because Stuie was simply too young to answer a business call. But Russell, who was older than me by a year and 8 months, never took a call.

By time I was 5, Russell had developed a gait in his walking. It was his teachers in school who noticed it.

A visit to Dr. Guinta resulted in my family's journey down a long, sad road. Frank Guinta knew what was wrong, but he needed such a life changing diagnosis confirmed.

So Daddy drove Mom, both Russell and Stuie, and me in his brown Dodge to the Children's Hospital in Boston. But Daddy was driving badly. He was very nervous.

As a child, his family had a summer house down in Warwick Neck, near Rocky Point Park. Their summer neighbors had three sons, all in wheelchairs. Each summer, for three years in a row, one of the boys would be missing. It was never explained why, but everyone knew anyhow.

Daddy and Mom went into the inner examination room with Russell while I stayed with Stuie. We played with what I thought were great toys, and we actually were having fun.

Anita did not accompany us. At 15, Anita could have outbursts. She didn't always, but sometimes, if she got mad enough, she could. This was obviously already a stressful situation for both my parents.

Daddy could often calm Anita down. He was the only one to call her Nina as a nickname. But, Daddy was so upset that he would have likely not have had the patience he usually had with his eldest child and oldest daughter.

Mom and Daddy came out without Russell, as blood work and urine samples were taken. The clinic found that nervous parents make it harder on the child to endure the actual testing.

Russell walked out with that gait, but he seemed unconcerned, maybe even cheerful. The technician and Russell spoke about the Red Sox, a subject Russell loved and knew much about.

He and his best friend, Dennis, swapped baseball cards often. And they, with other neighborhood boys, played baseball in our big backyard. Daddy and Russell watched the games in our den during summer evenings. Uncle Abe, Mom's brother, took us to a game at Fenway Park, all three of us, Russell, Stuie, and me. There was another trip to Boston' Children's Hospital for my family. Daddy drove even worse this time. We had been there before, but Daddy got lost. He stopped at the red light to roll down the window. The polite stranger gave him directions on how to go. Daddy couldn't keep the details straight in his mind.

I had heard the directions clearly so I proceeded to tell Daddy, step by step, how to get there. Daddy seemed even relieved that I could help him. Mom just let the events unfold because her mind was too cluttered to concentrate.

Russell, believe it or not, remained calm. He trusted that his parents and the experts could help him.

Stuie was just too young to comprehend that his future could also be impacted by the information we were about to receive.

Upon arrival, my parents were ushered into a conference room rather quickly. I could only glimpse the room briefly, but I saw a long table with a few people sitting behind it.

It was at least an hour before anyone entered the waiting room. It was a social worker who came to chat with me. Of course, she gave no details of anything discussed in the meeting. She just asked a few simple questions about Stuie, how old he was, and what he liked to play. That was it.

It was still some time before my parents came to take us home. Daddy was in rough shape. He was shaking. Mom seemed detached, as if she wasn't really living in the moment.

There was no talk of what was said at all. We got in the car and drove the 50 miles back home.

But Mom began to act clingy towards Russell. My older brother fell frequently. He didn't make a fuss about it. He wanted a bandage to cover the wound on his knee. But Mom made a big deal about it. Russell sometimes got his own bandage because he didn't want Mom to know he fell.

My parents began to argue sometimes. It was always about Russell. Daddy apparently disagreed with Mom how to handle their new information about Russell.

We kids never got involved with that, at least not directly. Anita began to hit me. My parents were distracted and did not pay heed to my complaints about Anita. I began to handle the situation on my own. I scratched Anita's arm whenever she began her attacks on me. So it looked like I was the troublemaker.

Oddly, Mom just said she would cut my finger nails to solve the problem. I was never punished.

Luckily, Anita was not home much. She volunteered to stack books at the school library, even though she never read any books on her own. She had a friend, Sharon, in the neighborhood.

Sharon was a very bright high school student who took on Anita as a friend. Anita went just down the street to see her. Anita had school friends who overlooked Anita's limitations. And she began to make friends with elderly people.

So my problem with her was not a constant one. I had a bigger crisis develop. I noticed Stuie did not walk as well as he should have. I just observed him at first. He was still 2 years and 8 months younger than me. Maybe he was just clumsy, as little children often are.

So I said nothing to my parents for awhile.

When I entered First Grade, I could not concentrate on my work. I was a poor student from the start. I also had a speech impairment that needed to be addressed. A speech therapist took me out of class to work with me. The other kids noticed that, and made fun of me.

My parents were generous people so I went to them to ask whether I could not be helped at home instead with my speech. They agreed immediately, and hired Mrs. Kirshenbaum.

She came from Montreal, Canada, to train in her profession. She married a lawyer, and they had a daughter named Marlene, a girl my age.

I often asked about Marlene. I wanted to meet her.

Mrs. Kirshenbaum made a deal with me. I was to work harder on my lessons with her. Then, she would take me to her home in Dean Estates to spend a few hours with her daughter.

So one Saturday, I was driven by Daddy to this fancy home. He would pick me up later. Marlene answered the door wearing an outfit I envied. She ushered me into her beautiful bedroom. The bed had a canopy over it. I had never seen that before. She had a very clean carpet in her room, and a big play area with miniature table and chairs for her to play on. And then I saw it! AN EASY BAKE OVEN!

I had seen one advertised on television commercials. But now I wanted one for myself.

Then my speech therapist came in to the room to offer us a treat. We followed her to the beautiful modern kitchen. On the kitchen bar were ice cream in special bowls you see at Woolworth's ice cream fountain. There were colorful sprinkles on top.

My reaction was totally the opposite of what it should have been. I began to cry. Her husband ushered Marlene out of the room. Mrs. Kirshenbaum hugged me and asked me to tell her why I was crying.

"Why can't I have a life like this?! My parents worry about Russell all the time. They yell sometimes at each other. I don't have a nice bedroom either, not even an Easy Bake Oven!"

She just held me, with no judgment. When I was ready, she let go of me. Marlene came back to have the ice cream with me.

Daddy came to pick me up at the appointed time. Nothing at all was said in front of me of what had happened.

But then Hanukkah came. My parents didn't usually give presents. We lit brightly colored Hanukkah candles each night. Stuie, Russell, and I stood around the table, as Mom sang songs in many languages. I loved that part the best. I was so proud that my Mom was so smart.

She made latkes, which my brothers ate. I didn't like them very much. Uncle Abe often brought chocolate cake for our Friday Sabbath meal so I would eat that instead.

But on this particular Hanukkah, Daddy told me to go in the car with him. He had a surprise for me. He drove me to Brodsky's toy store on Reservoir Avenue. We walked towards the boxes of Easy Bake Oven. He picked one up, then we headed to the register for him to buy it for me.

"Daddy, thank you so much!"

He seemed emotional about it. The owner noticed and came up to me. "Your father is a good man!"

I nodded in agreement. The owner handed me cake mixes created to use for the Easy Bake Oven.

"Happy Hanukkah, little girl! These are my presents to you."

Daddy offered to pay for them, but the owner refused payment for the cake mixes.

We went home where I immediately used the oven after using a mix for a batter. Daddy, my Mom, both my brothers, gathered around me. For once, I felt like a normal child celebrating our Jewish holiday.

Chapter 3:

An End to Innocence

 The following year, Stuie's walking got worse. I just couldn't keep quiet any more. I went to my parents to share my opinion.

  "Stuie is walking funny like Russell!"

It happened so fast how Mom reacted.

She slapped me across the face.

My Mom had never hit me before in my life. So I was just so shocked.

 Daddy got angry at Mom, "Tina!"

 Russell had seen the whole thing

 He rushed to my side, then hugged me.

Mom was sorry immediately. I let her hug me.

  "Little bird, I promise that won't happen again. Mommy was so wrong to do that to you!"

Anita happened to be there as well and laughed her head off. Daddy sent her to her room.

 Little Stuie sat on my lap as he often did.

"Ella", the name he often called me, "I love you!"

Mom broke down in tears, and rushed upstairs to the master bedroom.

Daddy sat down next to me. He quietly said, "Russell has Duchenne Muscular Dystrophy. Mom was just upset because we don't know if Stuie will get it, too!"

Duchenne Muscular Dystrophy would be said many times during my childhood and youth. I did not yet know the significance it would play in all of our lives. I didn't want to ask Daddy any questions right then.

Instead, I blurted the term out to my teacher, Mrs. Anderson. She ushered me out into the hallway.

"Cindy, this must be very hard on you and your family. I am sorry. But don't mention it in class again. You can talk to me about it privately, if you wish."

I had no idea why I couldn't talk about it in class.

Russell still played baseball in the yard with his friends for awhile longer. But he was no longer able to steal a base or slide into home base.

Suddenly, Russell stopped playing baseball. Daddy began to watch the games on television with Russell even more frequently than before. Dennis still came over to talk sports and trade baseball cards with my brother.

I continued to not only be a poor student, but to be bullied more in the schoolyard. I would come home crying sometimes.

Uncle Abe usually visited us on Friday, after work, and share the Sabbath meal with us. He brought a chocolate cake from Guttin's Bakery. Abe could not drive so he took a bus from work in Pawtucket to Downtown Providence. He then got on another bus bound for Cranston. Guttin's Bakery was on the corner of Park and Pontiac Avenue. He made his purchase there then took a short walk to our house.

Abe spoke with a strong Viennese accent. But his words were kind. He wanted to know about all of our day. Stuie and Russell told him good things. Stuie learned how to read very quickly. Russell talked about the Red Sox winning or losing. I told him a bully pushed me in the school yard.

One day, I came home hurt. Someone shoved me and I fell. My dress was ripped, my knee was bloody. I just cried so hard for awhile. Mom cleaned my knee and said she would buy me a new dress. Russell vowed to talk to his friends to find out what happened. Daddy offered to match down to that school to tell the principal.

The next day was a Thursday. Yet Abe was at my house. He told me he was taking me Downtown on the bus. I eagerly went with him. First, he took me to a watchmaker who spoke like Abe did. Abe bought me a fine watch to wear at school. Then, he brought me to a fancy restaurant. I could order anything I wished.

The next day, I wore my watch to school. In the school yard, I was made fun of. This time, I had something to say.

"Uncle Abe bought me this watch. I bet your parents won't

buy you something nice like this at all. You get a cheap, fake watch!" Then I stuck my tongue out.

No, I was never popular in the schoolyard, at recess. But there was no more physical conflict anymore. If I got hurt, it was because I was clumsy. I got picked last for gym teams, and few kids even talked to me.

Mom made going to the dentist a fun time. Mom took Stuie, Russell, and me Downtown on the bus. We changed the bus to go to Hope Street. Dr. Rubinstein was a pediatric dentist. He made the dentist chair go up by touching my nose. He had a great play area for us to wait our turn.

But the best part was after we had our check up and teeth clean. We took a bus Downtown Providence, but we didn't go home immediately. We stopped to do luncheon at Shepherd's Tearoom. Mom let us order whatever we wished to eat. I always had Boston Cream Pie with white filling.

We were happy being with Mom, together, the three of us children. We got along well with each other, and we loved our Mom. She was so cheerful and generous. She told us that her big sister, Regina, often took her for Sacher Torte after school.

Regina had died even before Russell was born. He was actually named for her with his first name. Anita had known Regina, and had loved her. But we three never had her in our lives.

We had Uncle Abe and Aunt Mina. Abe bought us cake, took us to a baseball game in Boston. He conducted our Passover Seders, and gave me a new watch.

Later, my relationship with Uncle Abe expanded. He was to have an even more positive, bigger role in all of our lives.

Aunt Mina was mentally ill. When we were very young, she came for Sabbath meal as well as Thanksgiving. She wore very long skirts, even in summertime, and always wore a hat on her head. She mumbled words in a mixture of German and Yiddish. Abe and Mom understood her, but we kids rarely did.

Anita actually made fun of Mina. My sister had been close Aunt Regina. But Regina had spoken good English. Regina could calm Anita. She helped fold laundry for Mom when they lived in South Providence, then played with Anita.

Regina died of a ruptured appendix in August of 1957. Anita lost an aunt who seemed to understand her needs well. But Aunt Mina was lost in a past world.

Chapter 4:

A Brief Ray Of Sunshine

I went into the third grade, feeling down. Russell's walking had got progressively worse over the course of three years. Our elementary school had a first floor as well as an upper level. 4th through 6th grade classes were located upstairs.

Russell was required to attend a one floor elementary school located across town. The City of Cranston had a driver who was to take him daily to and from his new school. He was sad to leave his friends, but he quickly made new friends. His adjustment was a good one.

But, Russell had been my popular older brother at my school. He convinced a few to at least leave me alone. He looked out for me, when he could.

I expected third grade to be a miserable experience for me. I was still a poor student. But Miss Gail Enos was a different kind of teacher. She considered the whole child, not just if the student was smart or not. She took me under her wing. She still had to grade my papers accordingly. Yet, she wanted to hear what I had to say. I could tell her I was sad about Russell being in a new school. That I was worried Stuie was coming down with Muscular Dystrophy. I shared about how much I liked my Easy Bake Oven, or that Uncle Abe took me out to eat at nice restaurants sometimes.

Then there was Clayton Prince Brown. That really was his name. I liked him. Not only was he cute, he was smart. Best of all, he was a kind boy. Clayton talked to me. He was also a good listener. Clayton did not let anyone bully me while he was around. He sat with me at recess, and at lunch.

I caught the measles that year. I was very sick and missed much school. Mom took good care of me. Stuie was already in school by this time. So Mom brought me tea in bed, then sat with me. She let me ask her a few questions about her childhood in Vienna. We could not talk about the Holocaust. She was ready to discuss that yet. But she did share how her sister, Regina, took her by trolley to school each day. That sometimes after school, her sister treated her to Sacher Torte at a cafe. Her father brought her to the opera house on special occasions. And her sister, my Aunt Mina, went to Prater Park with her to ride the ferris wheel. Uncle Abe, her brother, played chess and soccer, but he used an assume name to play on Saturday, the Jewish Sabbath, as not to shame their father, a Hebrew teacher.

She briefly spoke of her hard work in school, her goal was to become a doctor. But that she was thrown out of school when the Nazis arrived in Vienna.

She would say nothing beyond that time.

When I finally returned to school, Miss Enos welcomed me back with a hug. Clayton also hugged me. I had been missed by them.

But then Clayton told me his family was moving from Cranston to Foster when summer began. I ran home crying. He was really my best friend, and I was about to lose him!

Mom immediately got on the phone with his mother to invite Clayton over for dinner. Mom was not much of a cook, but she did her best. Daddy and my brothers were very friendly towards our guest. Anita went over Sharon's house for dinner when she was given the choice to be polite, or not be there.

It was Shabbat Dinner so Uncle Abe was there was well. Clayton respected Abe greatly. And Abe was his usual charming self. They talked alone in a corner for quite some time.

The year was coming to an end and my birthday fell just before the beginning of school summer vacation. Abe had a surprise in store for me. He was paying for my classmates to come for a birthday bash at my favorite restaurant. I wasn't sure who would accept this invitation. Many of them did. I know Clayton, as a popular kid, had something to do with that.

So Daddy took many trips to drive children to the restaurant. Of course, my brothers attended, as did my Mom. Clayton sat next to me at the party. There was dinner, which everyone ordered whatever they wished. Then there was birthday cake with ice cream as well as many presents.

It was a final, very happy memory in my childhood. My generous Uncle Abe made it possible, as did my friend, Clayton. I turned 9 at my very special party.

Chapter 5:
Troubles

Stuie's walking had worsened, but my parents avoided the testing for a final determination.

Then came the Muscular Dystrophy holiday event. Mom had begun to be active in the Rhode Island Chapter of the Muscular Dystrophy Association. We began to attend events as a family, all except Anita. Although Anita began to volunteer at the telethons Jerry Lewis started nationwide. She would do tasks for the organizers such as set up tables, make signs, greet other volunteers.

But she was not there at this holiday function held at a hall with some steps. There were helpers to lift identified patients such as Russell. But Stuie was yet to be listed as such.

During the event, Stuie went to the bathroom. Suddenly, everyone heard a terrifying scream! Stuie had fallen down the stairs and was bleeding. Mom administered first aid, but she exclaimed a rescue squad needed to be summoned at once.

The event was to be continued, as Mom accompanied Stuie in the rescue squad. I had no part of that. I was very upset. I told people that Stuie had Muscular Dystrophy. I basically shouted it, to make people listen to me.

Daddy took me aside.

"Cindy, I know. Mom needed more time to accept it."

"Can we stop pretending now?!", my face flooded with tears.

"Yes, we can", Daddy said gently.

Stuie was brought back with Mom in a taxi. He had a few bruises bandaged up. I hugged my little brother.

Stuie hugged me back. He whispered in my ear, "I have Muscular Dystrophy, Ella."

"We don't have to whisper, Stuie, anymore."

Stuie actually smiled,"Good."

Fourth Grade was a disaster. Mrs.W. was insensitive to my family's issues. She remarked that my dress was too short. I didn't try hard enough. That I should be kept back next year.

Daddy marched down to that school to confront the teacher. The principal got involved. Finally, it was decided I needed to see a child psychiatrist. My parents agreed, only if I would be promoted to the next grade. They said I had yet to blossom, but I would when I had a better teacher to guide me.

My psychiatrist was a woman. It was felt women were better suited to be a pediatric specialist. There were toys to play with, furniture my size to sit on. She spoke calmly, listened carefully. I saw her for a total of two months.

In the end, she wrote her report about me. My parents received a copy, as did the principal. I was promoted to 5th grade as promised. I did not require medication at all.

When my parents left the report in their bedroom, I sneaked into their room while Stuie was my look out, to warn me if someone was coming. Nobody was.

My reading skills weren't the best, but I had enough word knowledge to let me know what the psychiatrist thought was wrong with me. The words, deep grief, insensitive teacher, Russell and Stuie, Anita, were written. She wrote that any normal child would have deep emotions about what was happening.

The word "normal", seemed odd to me. I didn't feel normal at all. But at least, I was going into 5th grade, and would be rid of this teacher for good.

In 5th grade, my new teacher was neutral about me. Again, I was graded poorly, but I was treated fairly. This teacher did not embarrass me or make me feel badly about myself. I already felt terrible on my own.

Russell was now in a wheelchair. Stuie's walking just got worse everyday. Russell had an operation to extend his walking for two years. Stuie's spine could not be temporarily improved, whereas, Russell's heel cord had been stretched to give it a longer useful function.

And there was so much more involved with caring for Russell now. He had to be lifted in and out of chairs, carried upstairs, dressed and undressed, put on the toilet, given his books, plates, and silverware.

Stuie fell frequently now. He could still walk, but barely. I came home one day to be told Stuie was in the hospital for a bad cough. I slump into my chair. Mom served me supper, but I couldn't eat it, not at all.

At school, I threw away my recess snack. A few kids came up to me to say they hoped Stuie would be okay. I knew he would never be okay again. None of us would, not even Anita.

Because although Anita wished I had never been born, she wished our boys well. She even lifted Russell sometimes, to help him, or picked Stuie up after he fell.

One time, Anita asked to take Stuie on the bus Downtown, just to have a bite to eat. Anita knew how to take the bus, to be in a restaurant, to pay a bill, to make sure Stuie was safe. My parents agreed. Anita had only shown good intentions towards our brothers. She could be trusted.

Everything had gone fine. Anita took Stuie on the bus, sat next to him, held onto him on bumpy roads. She lifted him down the high step. They ate at a eatery near the bus stop. Stuie ate what he wished.

They got on the bus home. As they approached their stop, the bus driver carelessly opened the door too soon. Stuie went flying, but not before Anita wedged herself in front of him. She took the fall onto the pavement, saving Stuie's life.

Two passengers got off to help. One carried Stuie home, the other helped Anita walk.

Daddy rushed both Anita and Stuie to the hospital. Stuie was unharmed. Anita was hurt. She twisted her leg badly. She would walk badly for a few months. Even I felt sorry for Anita. She had been nothing less than heroic. Stuie shortly after ended up in a wheelchair. I found I could not eat much. My weight dropped 10 pounds. Dr. Guinta was alarmed. He told me parents to feed me anything I would eat.

Uncle Abe was enlisted to take me out to dinner more frequently. Mom let me go for hot wieners more often because I would eat them.

But my weight continued to go down.

I was now in 6th grade. My teacher took me aside one time, not to scold me, but to tell me about her brother. They lived in Scotland, but went on holiday in England. The hotel was by a swimming lake. She and her brother went into the water. She came out, but her brother didn't. She screamed for help, and many came. They found her brother, but it was too late. She blamed herself for years. She went to college, married, but never had kids. Fear stopped her. She was happy with her husband, but then he died. She was friendly with her nephew. She enjoyed being with a young person. She regretted that guilt stopped her from having her own children.

Her brother drowned because he suffered from epilepsy. He had a disease. It wasn't her fault at all.

My teacher said nothing more to me.

But the lesson, well said, had been wasted on me.

Chapter 6:

Wide Open World

Mom and Abe decided they were going to return to Vienna in 1972. It would be their first time back since the Holocaust. They consulted with Daddy and decided I would accompany them.

The logistics were rather complicated. The boys needed to be cared for. Both were in wheelchairs by now. The trip would take place at the end of the school year.

The boys would attend the Muscular Dystrophy Association Camp in Bedford, New Hampshire, for two weeks. A staff well trained to care for them were there 24 hours a day. A camp nurse was always available, a doctor was on call. Daddy would stay in Rhode Island, to drive to New Hampshire should any urgent situation come up.

On my actual birthday, Daddy took me to United Camera, to buy me one to take pictures of my trip to London, Vienna, and

Naples. He told me that I could learn much about Mom and Uncle Abe's past during this time. Maybe they would begin to answer my questions. I had so many they would not address.

Daddy's army troop had helped to liberate Dachau Concentration Camp in 1945. What he saw that day, and the days that followed, were implanted in his mind forever. He had told me what had happened, described it to me in graphic detail.

Thus, my interest in the Holocaust began. Daddy encouraged it. Maybe he did not know I ventured into my parents' bedroom, and searched for documents Mom had hidden. I found a few of them. Some were written in German, others in Italian. The one written in English caught my attention. She was in a place called Fort Ontario.

But she would not tell me anything at all at first. Abe only talked about the bike he rode, and that he ran over Mom's toes by mistake. That is why Mom had a crooked toe.

Now, we were to fly to London first, to see her childhood friend, Elsa. It was a long flight for me, made longer by the time difference. Upon arrival, I was so tired. Elsa's husband got the car from the parking garage at Heathrow Airport. Someone carried me.

We were driven to their home in Kensal Rise, in London. Once there, I slept on our hosts' bed for 6 hours. When I finally woke up, it was teatime. Elsa served tea, Earl Grey of course, miniature sandwiches, scones, and Sacher Torte.

Sacher Torte, that famed Viennese dessert, that Mom spoke of, was in front of me! I ate it all, every bite of it. Mom was so pleased. My eating had been poor since Stuie stopped walking.

Mom and Abe wanted to speak German to Elsa. That was their native language in Austria. But Elsa could not bear to say a word in German. So they used English.

I asked Elsa why she would not converse in German. So she

told me simply, "Mummy, Daddy, and my little brother perished in a concentration camp. My sister and I had work permits for England. We became maids. We survived the bombings. I met Bobby here. We changed his last name to make it sound English after we married. We raised our daughter here, and now she will have her family in England someday "

I pressed for more, but Mom changed the subject. Off to Windsor Castle tomorrow, the Tower of London the next day. But we would dine at a Swiss Restaurant tonight.

There was so much more to learn here. But it was for another time, when I came to England alone, without Mom and Uncle Abe.

The pilot from British Airlines who flew us into rainy Vienna apologized to my Mom and Uncle Abe for such a homecoming. But it was actually quite appropriate considering the circumstances that caused them to leave.

We hopped into a taxi where Mom and Abe easily spoke to the driver in German. I had no idea whatsoever what was said. We drove through the major streets where I saw beautiful old buildings mixed in with new modern ones.

But I had images of Jews' having their businesses burnt to the ground, the glass of synagogues shattered, with Torahs desecrated by being unrolled and ripped to pieces. And I saw a youthful Uncle Abe being dragged away to prison.

The dark mood I felt was broken when we entered the lobby of the Sacher Hotel. It was grand in an old world sense that America can not offer. There was a positive sense of history here. I learned Franz Sacher, the baker who first created the cake, had been Jewish. He had been privileged to make desserts for Prince Metternich. He gained the ability to operate a hotel because of royal protection.

Until the Nazi rule descended upon Vienna, and all Austria,

the Sacher Hotel was operated by his family through the generations.

After the war, American military personnel had run of the hotel, and Austrians were not permitted to enter at all as punishment.

The hotel returned to hosting the elite. Mom and Uncle Abe felt they deserved to stay at the Sacher, and they wanted to make my visit special as well. Mom and I had a grand suite, while Abe had a separate room from us. It was an old fashioned elevator that led us up and down into the great lobby.

We sat in the cafe, with its spotlessly clean table cloth and very proper wait staff. We had Wiener Schnitzel for our entree and Sacher Torte with whipped cream on the side. Everything was elegant, and quite Viennese.

The next day, Mom's friend, Rosie, and her husband, Fritz, picked us up in their car. First, pleasure before pain. We went to the Prater Park, where the couple's daughter, Brigette, rode with me on the rides.

Later, we visited Schonbrunn's Palace. We strolled through the gardens and took pictures by the water foundations.

We ate together in the revolving restaurant called Donauturm. But Abe seemed troubled. He stared out at the Danube River belong. Usually very personable, he seemed rather withdrawn. Mom advised me to let him be.

The next day, it had been planned that I stay with Brigette while the adults went to the neglected Jewish Cemetery. But I refused to be left behind, so I went, too!

What I saw was very overgrown grass that was taller than I was at the time. Fritz had cutters in hand to get us through.

We saw my great-grandparents gravestones first. They were Mom's paternal grandparents. She had known them rather well. They had lived with her family during early childhood.

He had died in 1935. But she had died in 1938. Questions swerved in my brain about her death. But I said nothing at the time. And then we moved on to two spots with a simple marker to label the space number.

"What is this?", I blurted out.

Mom said, "This is where Uncle Lazar and Klara are buried!"

"Why don't they have gravestones?", I demanded to know.

Abe got upset with me. Usually always patient and kindly with me, he snapped, "This place is not for you to be!"

I became upset, "Why not? This is my family history, too, and I have a right to know what it is!"

We just left the cemetery at that point. Mom then said to her brother, "Abe, she is just curious, that's all. She is a child, after all."

Abe said nothing at all. He seemed very nervous, on edge, and completely ill at ease.

We went on to the apartment where they at once lived, in the 9th district. But Abe would not go beyond the courtyard. So Mom and I went without him. Mom knocked at the door of her former home.

Mom inquired in German to the woman who answered that since she once lived there, long ago, could show show me the inside?

The word Juden was uttered in a unfriendly voice among other words spoken. The door was slammed in our faces. We returned to where Abe stood waiting for us.

"The lady slammed the door in our face!", I exclaimed.

Abe responded, "This courtyard is where the Nazis dragged me away to prison!"

Mom added, "The woman said she thought Hitler killed all the Jews. She seemed sorry he hadn't."

Abe answered, "I expected that reception. These people would kill us now, if they could!"

I began to shake. Mom took me by the hand when we saw a boy on a bike who laughed at me. Abe said something in German to him that made him be quiet and ride off in great haste.

That night, in our hotel room, I screamed in my sleep that the Nazis had come for us.

Next day, Brigette and her parents came to say farewell. Brigette presented me with a box. Inside was a miniature ferris wheel of the one we rode in the Prater.

I liked the gift, but I was glad to leave Vienna for now. But I knew I would be back someday. I had much unfinished business here.

We flew into Rome from Vienna on Austrian Airlines. We were supposed to transfer onto a short flight on Al Italia Airlines into Naples, but it was delayed 6 hours! So we got into a cab where Mom spoke Italian to the driver. We were off so Mom could get her hair done.

Abe and I went for gelato at a nearby cafe by the hair salon. He seemed relax now that we were in Italy. We walked around and made friends with police. They posed in a picture with us.

Mom was finally done so a cab was called to take us back to the airport. The flight finally took us to Naples.

Mom's old friend, Benjamin, picked us up in his car. His adult son accompanied him. We squeezed in the back and we drove off at a fast speed.

We met his wife and other adult children. The wife seemed unhappy we were there while the sons were hospitable to us.

Benjamin and his older son drove us to our hotel by the sea. Mom and Benjamin seemed to have alot to talk about. Mom looked out at the water a lot, but said nothing in English.

We were taken around Naples. It looked dirty and ancient to me. We walked around a castle and stopped at a cafe. I ordered chocolate cake, but after eating some of it, I felt very dizzy. We went back to the hotel immediately. Mom told them I was unwell. It was asked what I had eaten. My mother said chocolate cake. The response was there was rum in that cake! I never had liquor before that day so I was unaccustomed to having any! In other words, I was drunk!

A good night's sleep restored me to better balance again.

There was something about Mom's connection to Naples I had yet to understand. The day would come when I learned what it was. But it was not to be on this trip.

When we arrived back to Boston, Daddy awaited our arrival to Logan Airport. He hugged Mom, then me. He was glad we were back.

We would get our boys from camp in a couple of days. Meanwhile, Mom rested to get ready to resume care for two boys in wheelchairs. I entered 7th grade with a greater vision. I had to wear glasses for board work, but I also learned that Europe had beckoned to me to return, to find more answers to my many questions.

Chapter 7:
Awakening

Suddenly, I became a good student. I was again in the same school as Russell was. This junior high had an elevator that allowed my older brother access with his wheelchair. He had a helper with him, a fellow student who volunteered.

But this school also had some Anti-Semitism that came with a few students. J.C. made fun of my last name and called me a dirty Jew. No one corrected him.

Other student copied off my test paper.

My work was good despite the constant torment I suffered. I met another girl named Rose. She was a foster child. That was the reason why she was picked on. So we became friends. It was us against the world.

The teasing was relentless for both of us. We were outcasts for being different.

Daddy went down to that school many times on my behalf. Mom called parents of bullies to inform them of what their children were doing.

But Russell, as before in his other schools, remained popular. A girl wanted to go with him to a school dance. So Daddy picked her up with Russell in the car. Daddy unloaded the wheelchair and dropped them off at the event. A few hours later, Russell called. His date had disappeared. Daddy came at once and discovered the date was getting high in the bathroom. He took her home immediately to parents who did not care.

But Russell remained hopeful and optimistic about life. This experience did not bring him down.

I never had any boy like me in 7th or 8th grade. I did my work, and went home. But at least Rose was my friend. We took her to a holiday party for Muscular Dystrophy. She won the raffle and got a prize. She was pleased. She also had a crush on Russell.

In 9th grade, I was to be in a Christmas play. I had no idea what to do for a costume. I tried my best to throw one together. The drama instructor screamed at me. I cried back, "I am a Jew. How would I know what to wear?"

Suddenly a boy named Allen put his arms protectively around me and exclaimed, "We Jews will stick together! "We each had not known the other was Jewish. We never dated, even once, and would never be a couple. But on that one occasion, he was my knight in shining armor.

Daddy took me to a costume store to buy me period appropriate attire for a herald.

Chapter 8:
Vienna Again

That year, Abe took me to Vienna with my sister, Anita. Anita had been kicked out of the house a few years before on my account. She was caught choking me by the neck, and made to leave. She had a full time job in a jewelry factory. She had moved in with Abe and Mina.

The time away from each other was good for both of us. She had promised never to harm me again.

In Vienna, Abe was working with the government to get the pension he paid in for as a young man. So Anita and I took a trolley to the shopping district.

Anita had heard both Yiddish and German spoken by our late Aunt Regina. I never knew Regina at all, but Anita was close to her until that aunt died when Anita was 7. Anita also knew our grandparents. They spoke German as well as Yiddish.

So because Anita was compromised, she mixed the two languages up, creating a language of her own.

Anita was a heavy young woman. We went into a department store where she expected to find her size. But it simply wasn't there. Anita attempted to speak to the sales clerk. The woman failed to be able to understand Anita at all. Anita felt the woman was just being rude to her. My sister got hostile very fast, raising her fists to the clerk.

Anita was in danger of being arrested in Vienna!

I asked the woman if she spoke English? She did! I told her if we left, would she not make trouble? The woman said if we departed immediately, then the police would not be called.

I told Anita in no uncertain terms that she needed to go with me now, or be arrested!

Anita believed me somehow. I took the money Abe gave us for shopping to pay for a cab back to our hotel. I ordered apple strudel for Anita to eat to calm her down.

Chapter 9:
Stuie and School

I entered the 10th grade, leaving Bain Jr. High School behind, and beginning three years at Cranston High School East. Russell attended Cranston West because it was more accessible to him. East had two buildings, with City Hall separating the two. The main building had flights of steps with no elevator.

Stuie started at Bain. He was in the 7th grade. My little brother's advanced intelligence was apparent early as. Even as he stumbled and fell because of rapidly weakened muscles, his mind soared. He could grasp new concepts, develop his knowledge, and expand upon them.

Stuie didn't just rely on teachers to learn, he became self-taught at home. He studied German, wrote drills and practice exercises. He explored science, and organized his findings about the Stock Market. He learned the state capitals of every state, read about geography, coined coins.

But I became his biggest project of all. As I gained footing in my studies in 7th grade, he wanted to keep me moving in the right direction. He encouraged me to study hard, to do my homework, and set long term goals for myself. He believed in me, but he wanted me to believe in myself.

That was the hard part of course. Being made fun of at school, even after achieving good grades finally, having my sister show great dislike for me, my brothers both declining physically, really ate away at my self- confidence.

Stuie gave me the drive to overcome some of my own doubts. He had fewer friends at school than Russell. Stuie's clothes bunched up in the back from his curving spine, so he even looked different, beyond being in a wheelchair. He was smarter than his classmates, and Stuie wasn't afraid to show it.

Stuie's teachers respected his abilities, but didn't always understand his needs. His quietness, to them, meant that he was okay. But he wasn't. He needed more cushions, as he was hunched over. He required repositioning often. His coughs were labored during head colds.

But Stuie stayed within himself, to conquer what Muscular Dystrophy took away from him.

There was a cruel boy at school, likely Anti-Semitic. Stuie was openly Jewish, stating what he believed, and what he celebrated. The boy threatened to throw Stuie down the stairs in his wheelchair.

The Assistant Principal got word of this threat and confronted the tormentor. He lost his temper with someone threatening a wheel bound student. He said if any harm came to Stuie, he would come looking for him. The veiled threat was clear.

But even well meaning classmates hadn't a clue how much Stuie was suffering with his disease. Stuie declined faster than Russell did. And Stuie, being scientific minded, faced his own death.

He told my parents he wanted a blue casket. I thought he was talking about some distant future. I was in total denial. Stuie also worried about me. Stuie was always a saver. The Bar Mitzvah money he received was tucked away in a bank account. But he wanted more money for me to have. He talked my parents into making me the benefactor of an insurance policy on him.

I never knew any of this. Perhaps my parents humored Stuie, when he made this request of them. Or maybe they realized he was dead serious.

Chapter 10:
Life Continues
 Meanwhile, life went on for all of us. Stuie achieved honors at school, and at the science fair held at Rhode Island Junior College.
 And Russell had become Poster Youth for the Muscular Dystrophy Association, Rhode Island Chapter. Mom was now volunteer Vice President for Muscular Dystrophy in Rhode Island. Their efforts were sometimes combined, but often separate duties.
 Mom needed beautiful gowns to wear at evening fund raising events. She sought her evening wear at Mrs. D's fashion boutique. Russell had to have suits and ties for his many speaking engagements.
 Russell's efforts led him to an appearance on Jerry Lewis' Telethon in Las Vegas. Both parents needed to accompany him. Uncle Abe came to stay with Stuie and me during their absence. Abe took us out to eat, let us eat sweets, and indulged us so we wouldn't feel badly that we couldn't be included in on the trip to Las Vegas.
 My Italian Class was going on a trip to Italy in April of 1976. I wanted to go, to be a part of something of my own, separate from anything to do with Muscular Dystrophy. Daddy understood that. But he had some hard decisions to make first.
 Russell's Italian Class at Cranston West was invited to join the trip Cranston East was going on. Russell, of course, wanted to go, too. Mom would also accompany him, to care for his many needs. Daddy had the money to sponsor all of us.

But I insisted it was my trip, not to be shared. Just as Russell had his trip to Las Vegas, this was mine alone.

Daddy wrestled with my desire to not have Russell go. Then, part of the trip fell during Passover. It obviously would not be followed.

In the end, Russell elected not to go. He could have insisted, but he didn't. He told Daddy to let me have this trip for my own.

I was still an unpopular girl, although I was now a good student. No one from my class wanted to be my roommate on the trip. Finally, a popular girl offered to share a room with me in the various hotels.

Our plane was suppose to land in Milan, but it was diverted to the tiny Trieste Airport, on the edge of the border with Yugoslavia. We could see the fence that separated us from a Communist country. Our chartered bus met us at the changed destination and drove us to our intended first stop, Venice.

My group toured Dogi Palace first. I still had my Instamatic camera from my first trip to Europe. Daddy had gifted it to me. So I was preoccupied with developing a picture I took. By time I looked up, my group was nowhere to be seen.

I wandered around La Piazza San Marco aimlessly. I was lost in a foreign country, with no fluency of the language, all alone. I wondered whether G-D was punishing me for not letting Russell come?

But a man spotted me and spoke English to me. He agreed to accompany me safely back to my hotel. We chatted as we walked, which slowed down the progress of our way back.

He asked me whether I was Catholic or Protestant? I responded that I was neither. A long pause followed. I decided to risk telling him I was a Jew.

His reaction was one of utter shock.

He quietly said, "So is my mother."

I added for good measure, "Mom survived the Holocaust in Italy."

His Mom had as well.

This connection between us was apparent. He held my hand. I am not sure that I was comfortable with the physical contact. But I let it continue.

We made it back to my hotel. Suddenly, he grabbed me and gave me my first kiss, then he was gone.

I entered the lobby, rather numb from what had just happened. My teachers and classmates encircled me. Their relief was quite visible.

"I dreaded calling your parents, to tell them you were missing", exclaimed Mr. Bruno.

Girls who had refused to be my roommates on the trip hugged me.

But no one asked me how I managed to get to the hotel, and I didn't offer to tell them. What had happened was my secret to hold onto, until I decided to let it be known.

We went on to Florence. Everyone kept a close watch on me, not wanting a repeat of what happened in Venice. We went to a disco. Ordinarily, no boys took notice of me back at school, except as friends. But here, I passed for Italian, with my dark hair and hazel eyes. The Italian males wanted to dance with me while beautiful blonde hair fellow students sat on the side, watching me dance.

So many in fact danced with me that night. Mr. Bruno practically had to drag me off the dance floor when it was time to return to our hotel. I had never experienced such popularity before, and I never would again. That evening in Florence was magical for me.

We went to the Tower of Pisa. Being vain, I didn't wear glasses during this trip. Going up the steps I did along side my classmates. Going back down was another matter entirely. The steps were blurred, and I felt why it was called the Leaning Tower of Pisa. A German speaking man of middle aged came along to help. All thoughts of him or his family having anything to do with the Holocaust vanished as he extended his hand to guide me down the many steps.

Chapter 11:
Stuie at Disney World
The following year, my theater class was traveling to England. I would be going, too. But this time, there were two trips being planned for two members of my family.

Stuie never asked for much from my parents. They often had to ask him what they could do for him. Finally, he had an answer for them. He wanted to go to Disney World. His wish was gladly granted, but not easily. Daddy was still affluent. He had the money to fund both trips. The problem was that not only did Russell need care while Mom was gone, but what obstacles Mom faced to care for Stuie, and take him where he needed to go.

Mom, as always, undertook solving problems with a strong will and a can-do attitude.

As my plane flew off from Logan Airport in Boston, heading towards England, another plane took off for Orlando, Florida. Mom had lifted Stuie out of his orange wheelchair and placed him into his plane seat, putting his seatbelt on. When the plane landed, she carried him out of his seat back into his wheelchair. She lifted him in the taxi cab while, hopefully, the driver put the wheelchair in the trunk.

At the hotel, Mom wheeled Stuie to dinner. She brought him back to the hotel room, undressed him, then put him in bed. She repositioned him in bed during the night. She bathed him in the morning, dressed him, took him to a shuttle to take then to Disney World. She lifted him up the stairs of the bus to seat him. She carried him down again, and placed him in his wheelchair.

She wheeled him all day. She lifted him on and off rides, took him to eat, then lifted him back up shuttle stairs.

They stayed all week while I was in England.

Meanwhile, Uncle Abe came to stay with Daddy and Russell. While Daddy worked, Uncle Abe lifted Russell from his bed after he dressed him. He carried him downstairs to give him breakfast. He turned on the radio for Russell to listen to. He took him out in his wheelchair to a restaurant to eat.

Stuie and Mom returned from their vacation, and I came back from my trip to England. Daddy brought Uncle Abe home and Abe went back to his paid job as Hasbro Toy Company.

Chapter 11:

Russell 's Dream Comes True, Mine Doesn't.

Russell had wanted to become a sportscaster since the time he stopped walking. The dream could only be realized with a college degree. My older brother was a straight C student so that presented a problem for admission.

A man named Michael Nordstrom, a Protestant gay minister, was a liaison for disabled students at Rhode Island College. He presented Russell's case before a board. Russell was much more than what his grades said he was. He had been a Poster Youth on behalf of Muscular Dystrophy. He delivered speeches, gave interviews, was in commercials, appeared once with Jerry Lewis in Las Vegas on the telethon. Although not scholastic like his younger brother, he, too, had competed in science fairs.

It was determined Russell's other merits deemed him acceptable for entrance to college. Daddy hired a full time helper to commute him and care for him during the day.

With Russell at college during the day, Stuie in 9th grade, and me a high school senior, Mom decided to volunteer at Roger Williams Hospital. She translated for patients who spoke no English as doctors diagnosed them. With Mom's medical knowledge, she could explain medical issues doctors evaluated.

I stepped up my game even more at school. Stuie worked hard with me to drill me on my Latin, Italian, Psychology, Economics, and English. I needed no assistance for European History. I was an excellent student in that subject.

I was applying to both top notch schools and Rhode Island local colleges. My goal was to get into Brandeis, to work towards advanced degree in Jewish European History. Daddy promised to pay for my undergraduate degree in history. He hoped I would pursue a legal degree after I obtained my Bachelor's Degree in history.

Mom and I took 5 buses to Waltham to visit Brandeis. My mother was displeased by the snobbish attitude she saw there. She did not think it could work for me.

I applied there, as well as at Clark, University of Rhode Island, and Providence College. I was rejected from Brandeis. My grades solid, my SAT scores were not.

During my SAT's, my mind wandered to visions of death and dying. I just couldn't concentrate well enough to do a good job.

Clark wait listed me. If I did a year elsewhere and did well, I could attend for my sophomore year.

I got accepted to both URI and Providence College. I turned URI's offer down. I would go to P.C., a Catholic College as a commuter student.

Russell had a few bumps in his freshman year of college. Mom had little knowledge of Sociology, but I was taking it in my second half of my senior year. So I tutored Russell in it. I feared my teaching fell short, Russell didn't grasp all the concepts. But he was passing at least, so Daddy said I did a good job.

Chapter 12:
Tragedy
Then everything changed on May 3, 1978 that affected everyone in my family, even Anita and Uncle Abe. As I walked home from school, a sense of horror seized hold of me. I ran towards my house, my heart beating fast. I entered the front door and screamed loudly, "Stuie is dead!"
A distant relative tried to hush me, as not to upset my parents. But our family friend, Katherine, brought me upstairs to express my grief.
Uncle Abe was there in the house, so was Anita. Daddy's relatives were present as well. Neighbors showed up, friends of the family.
But Russell had yet to come home from college for the day. As the car pulled up to the curb, Uncle Abe asked to have a word with Russell's helper before my brother was lifted in.
The helper was in shock, he collapsed on the chair. So Abe carried Russell into the house. It was Mom who broke the news to my now surviving brother.
Russell was speechless, perhaps for the first time in his life. Stuie was gone, dead from Duchenne Muscular Dystrophy. The same disease he had. Stuie had been only 15. Russell was closer to 20.
I have no idea what thoughts Russell had about his own fate. I was concentrating on my own terrible loss.
Katherine told me how events unfolded that day. Mom went downstairs to get Stuie's shoes. When she came back upstairs, Stuie was collapsed on the bed. He was not breathing. She

started CPR, screaming for Daddy to call the rescue squad. Daddy took over with CPR as Mom met the paramedics at the door. There was no pulse, but CPR was continued by both paramedics. They decided to transport anyhow.

Mom rode with them in the rescue squad. She waited for word in the reception area. A team of doctors worked on a dead boy. No matter what they tried, it failed. Stuie was dead.

Daddy got the call and went to the fire department. The fire chief drove him to Rhode Island Hospital.

At the hospital, the doctors asked for an autopsy. It would not bring him back, and it violated Jewish law.

My parents argued with the doctors, pleaded with them to release Stuie to the undertaker. Mom began to call people, anyone who would say that Stuie died from a terrible disease. The police chief knew Daddy, he helped raise money during telethons. The Mayor of Cranston came, vowed Stuie had been well cared for. The owner of Adler's Hardware appeared. She knew our family well.

It was agreed that no autopsy was needed. Sugarman's undertaker came in person, to take Stuie away from this doubt about his death. He drove him to the funeral parlor, to prepare him himself.

The rabbi was called. Uncle Abe was driven to our house by the owner of Hasbro Toy Company. Daddy's bail bondsman clients got word. Mafia wives came to clean the curtains, neighbors did laundry. Daddy's relatives brought food.

Anita was totally in grief as well. She cried for her little brother. She caught sight of me hysterical and in tears. This one time she reached for me, not in anger, but in compassion.

When I entered the funeral parlor to see Stuie's brown casket, I understood why. My parents asked me what was more important to Stuie, a blue metal casket or a Jewish funeral and burial? I said Stuie was a strong Jew. He kept the Passover, fasted on Yom Kippur, would only celebrate Hanukkah.

And so Stuie was dressed in white, with the prayer shawl he wore for his Bar Mitzvah, just 2 years before, and a yamulka on his head. He was placed in his casket by the man who got him from Rhode Island Hospital. The lit was open for Mom and Daddy to see Stuie one final time.

My friends from school, Rose and Howie, took me by the arm to steady me. They really had to lift me along, as my feet would not work.

I paid little heed to Russell. His many friends came. Abe stood ready as well. Michael Nordstrom bowed his head in Hebrew prayer. Anita's fellow workers were there. Russell's best friend, Dennis, mourned with his friend. Kids who could not come had their parents' be there in their place. The Mayor of Cranston, Daddy's lawyer friends, Judges Daddy appeared before for bail cases, all showed up.

Traffic jams on Route 95 to the cemetery formed.

Stuie's casket was lowered into the ground, the young rabbi trembling.

Chapter 13:

Upside Down

I was not okay.

Neither was Daddy.

Mom tried to be brave for Russell's sake.

Russell didn't say how he felt.

Anita had trouble doing her work.

Abe grieved for his little nephew.

Aunt Mina came to see us. It was unusual. She rarely ventured beyond Downtown Providence. But there she was. She held her younger sister's hand. She hugged her surviving nephew. She had a little box for me to have. Inside was miniature furniture she collected. She gave them to me to keep.

I somehow graduated from high school. I had good grades before Stuie died. I managed to hold onto most of them.

Daddy stopped talking to me. He seemed mad at me. I had no reason why. Mom took care of Russell, but argued with Daddy, this time about me. She told him he was bringing even more harm to me. He just ignored her. He was able to still be good to Russell. He talked to him, told him not to give up on himself, to keep going, to live, not to die.

So I worked that summer at Rocky Point Park. A guy came over to my game and spoke to me. We made a date. He brought me home to meet Mom and Russell. Daddy left the house to go for a walk.

6 weeks later, I wore an engagement ring on my finger. I was to be married the following June. Russell pleaded with Daddy to still pay my college tuition. Daddy promised he would. Then there was to be my wedding. Daddy threatened not to pay for it, or even to come.

Russell cried tears for me. Stuie was dead and Cindy might be next. Her grief is so bad, maybe she will join her little brother, too.

Daddy's wall came tumbling down. He asked me to go for counseling, I refused. He told me to go to college, no matter what. If I did, he would give me my Jewish wedding.

So I was married under the canopy by the rabbi who buried Stuie. After my wedding, the rabbi came to see my parents. He was quitting his position at the temple to work in his father's furniture business. Stuie's death had impacted him greatly. He questioned his fate and could not go on the pulpit any longer.

The following year of Stuie's death, my husband and I wanted to buy a small ranch. I would continue college while my husband worked. But we wanted to stop renting our third floor tenement.

Daddy and Mom told me to come visit them alone. I came, not knowing what to expect. Daddy placed in my hands a check for 5000 dollars. I thanked them for their help, but Daddy nodded no. The check was a gift from Stuie.

They explained how Stuie wanted me to inherit his money saved as well as the benefit on the small insurance policy. He wanted them to give it to me for something important. Buying a house was the right occasion for me to receive it. But Stuie unselfish gift did not have the desired results he wished for me. Although my husband bought me a puppy. I named her Terri. But he beat me and my dog. It could be she barked too loudly, I let the milk go bad. I said the wrong thing. He beat me in the yard once. He took his feet to kick me. Next, he got a stick, but Terri wouldn't let him. My dog laid on top of my fallen body, to shield me from the impact. A neighbor screamed at him to stop, or the police were to be called.

My parents' door was always opened to me, but I could not go back. Russell's fate was now clear to me. To watch him die was something I could not do.

I commuted to college, long sleeves and long pants covered my bruises. I liked Sociology like I did in high school. I had the most wonderful professor, Dr. Sarah Curwood, as my teacher. I still loved history. But I could only write about the Holocaust in a few papers. It was general European History as well as American History that was offered at Rhode Island College.

I had transferred out of Providence College. The work was too hard for me. Gone with my A's and B's, from high school honors, replaced by straight C's, except for one D.

At RIC, I had B's and C's. I wasn't so proud of myself, sad for Daddy, who wanted me to succeed, even go to law school. Mom took it in stride. As long as I graduated with an undergraduate degree, there was hope for something more, when I was ready.

Chapter 14:
Russell's Wish Comes True

But meanwhile. Russell got an exciting offer. Russell was

offered the opportunity he dreamt of from when he had to be in a wheelchair at age 12. He could be the sportscaster for the Rhode Island College Girls' Basketball Team.

Home games were no problem. I could drive Russell and Daddy to the college for the games. I would have to do the driving because our father stopped driving after Stuie died. He got in too many accidents. He considered himself an unfit driver now. However, Daddy had to go to lift Russell into his wheelchair from the car and back into the car again. If he had to use the toilet, Daddy had to take him. But there were games held at other schools. Granted, those colleges were either in Massachusetts or Connecticut, but we had to go on the chartered bus with the team. Daddy would have to lift Russell up the steep bus steps.

Daddy was 68 in 1980. He was in good shape. He jogged regularly, was an ideal weight, never smoked or drank. So he was able to lift Russell, who was a thin young man of 21. Yet, a man of Daddy's age could develop health concerns.

For now, at least, Daddy managed.

So I drove them to local games, and accompanied them on the bus for out-of-state ones. I was helpful to Daddy as an extra set of hands.

But one time, the bus driver got careless. Before anyone was on the bus to return to Rhode Island, the bus rolled. No driver was in sight. The bus inched towards parked cars. I screamed. Daddy sprung into action by leaping on the moving bus and turning the bus off.

Not bad for a man of his age.

So Russell struggled to graduate college on time in May of 1981. Professors and students urged Russell not to worry if he had to take longer to graduate. But my brother insisted he had to graduate with his class.

There were obstacles in his way. Cold winters were hard on

him as he had to be wheeled across campus. The wind could whip up and he might be very cold. It was feared that he would catch a cold. Russell's disease had progressed to the point that he had weakened muscles that could not cough up mucus. Pneumonia was a great threat to his life, should he ever develop it.

And odd assignments were hard for him to complete. Michael Nordstrom had advocated for Russell's special physical issues, but there were core requirements that could not be waved

So, one such assignment was to interview Narragansett Indians. I had to drive Russell to where they lived. He had to ask questions, observe the environment, then write a report. Mom had to type all his papers now. His fingers were too weak to type.

The Chief himself lifted Russell out of the car into warmer indoors. His wife wanted Russell to drink tea, not because of custom, but out of concern for the young man.

Russell got the report done. He was graded only a "C", but it was enough. We only stayed a short time with the tribe. Questions were rushed, answers jotted down by me. At this point, Russell's health was the focus.

But on a spring day, in May, Russell Chernick graduated college as a member of the Class of 1981. His CPA was a 2.02. He had to pass a math course in his final semester. Mom, a whiz in math, tutored him the best she could. In the end, he had to not just pass the test , he had to have a score of 80 to offset a previous test in which he scored poorly. Russell got an 88!

Russell, always a positive person, must have understood his situation more than we realized. He was right. He had to graduate that year with his class so his goal to receive a college degree was reached.

Chapter 15:
Another Loss

It was my senior year of college. The year was 1982. Just before spring vacation, I saw Russell in the RIC Library. He had graduated college that last May. But he took a couple of graduate courses in Counseling. He was not a matriculated student in the program. Russell could only be on campus a few days a week. But Russell needed stimulation of being with people. Being home all the time would depress a sociable person like Russell was.

I had a very brief conversation with my brother. It was pleasant enough. His helper was there to whisk him home. Temperatures had dropped, and Russell could not be about in such brisk weather.

I attended my last class before school break began. I went home as usual. My husband came home from work, I made dinner, then he went outside to fix his car.

I decided to take a warm shower. When I had just stepped on of it, the phone rang.

I picked up the phone and heard Mom speak. But she wasn't really talking, she was crying, "Hurry! Go to Rhode Island Hospital. It's Russell!"

I threw the phone down with a terrible bang.

I ran outside in my bathrobe, with no shoes on and screamed, "Russell is in danger! We must go to the hospital now!"

S responded immediately. Despite his cruelty towards me, he liked Russell as his brother-in-law. I just put clothes on and we sped towards Rhode Island Hospital.

Once there, I saw my Mom and Dad there with the doctor. The doctor explained, "It is grim. We had to cut his throat to place the breathing tube. We will need to run tests. You may as well go home. Doctors will be with him constantly to care for him."

So S and I walked silently with Mom and Dad to the parking lot. A neighbor came to take them home.

I later learned that Russell was up in his bedroom and cried out he could not breathe. Our parents rushed up to help him. But he had stopped breathing by then. Mom began to perform CPR while Daddy called the rescue squad.

Once again, the paramedics arrived. This time, unlike last time with Stuie, they got a pulse.

But as the rescue squad raced to the hospital, communications with doctors broke off. At that time, a drug to prevent brain death required specific permission. It could not be granted.

The question had to be answered. Was Russell now brain dead?

Russell survived the night, but there was no response from him to indicate that his brain had also lived.

Because of his youth, my brother was given repeated brain scans to be quite sure of the results.

The stem of his brain was the last to die. He had absolutely no brain waves at all.

The weather remained horrible. Mom and Daddy had to decide what needed to happen next. I sat by my motionless brother. I was very tired by now. I thought I fell asleep by his side. But I heard Russell's voice.

"Cindy, tell them to let me go."

I woke up startled. I saw Russell lying there, as before, with tubes running through him. I heard the machine he was attached to working to breathe for him. I looked into his eyes.

They opened sometimes, but they had a blank stare.

Mom and Daddy arrived for the visit.

I wiped my tears the best I could, then said, "My brother is dead!"

Daddy responded, "Well, he is gravely ill, but not dead."

"No, Daddy, Russell is dead. Only his body lives!"

Mom shook her head yes, but said nothing.

Michael Nordstrom showed up at that moment. Even through he was a Protestant Minister, he knew Hebrew Prayers.

"Michael, please recite the prayers of the dying for Russell!"

Michael looked to my parents to verify whether they wanted him to do this.

Daddy and Mom told him to go ahead.

The next day, I drove Daddy and Mom to sign the required papers needed to turn life support off.

"I feel like an executioner!", Daddy exclaimed.

I was struggling to find a parking spot. Someone grabbed the one I tried to get.

I lost my temper, got out, and screamed at the driver, "My brother is brain dead!"

He calmly responded, "So is my daughter."

I found another spot to park in.

The middle aged man walked up with us to ICU.

No words of wisdom were spoken. Deadly silence reigned. So Mom, Daddy, Uncle Abe, Michael Nordstrom, Anita, my best friend, Rose, my husband, and I all gathered to say good-bye to Russell.

I later learned Dennis, Russell's best friend, had come to say good-bye as well.

Mom decided when the plugs were removed next morning, we were not to be there. It was too painful. Russell would never know the difference.

Mom called me next morning to tell me Russell was now

dead. I don't remember the rest of my day at all.

What I do recall is what happened when S came home from work. I will not write the graphic details here in this book. But I would feel guilty for many years on Russell's Yahrzeit that I had to also remember being violated. The Yahrzeit would be compromised by what happened that same day.

Being wiser now, I realize that I had done nothing wrong. That blame must be placed where it belongs.

At Russell's burial into the cold ground, the wall that separated Stuie's grave from Russell's new resting place collapsed. It would be restored, but it was symbolic that our two boys, my brothers, briefly shared the same space. They both struggled with the same deadly disease. And they both will always share a special place in my heart forever.

Chapter 16:
College Graduation

Immediately thereafter, I had to go back to college. I had exams I had to take. I had not studied for them. The vacation had been used up by Russell's dying and death, the funeral and shiva.

I did badly on my English Literature Examination. I was in deep trouble. The teacher, a terrible man, warned me I had to get a B on my final to pass.

My Mom had something else on her mind. Russell's life had been a positive thing, and his death had to serve some good purpose as well. She asked her political friends to sponsor a bill that would allow paramedics discretion in case communications were lost with the hospital.

It was a fight to pass it. Private ambulance companies fought its passage. They feared it would result in law suits and loss of business.

A compromise was reached in the final hours. Private companies would be exempt. Only city and town rescue squads would use the bill.

The bill passed. Russell's death would hold meaning beyond our family's grief. Lives would be saved because Russell lost his.

Mom had time now to help me in my situation.

"Eat fish. It is brain food."

I listened, although I hated fish.

I studied hard.

I prayed.

Even Michael Nordstrom prayed on my behalf.

I got an 88 on my final English Literature Exam, just as Russell scored an 88 on his math exam the year before. Russell had graduated college because of that score, and so did I!

On May 22, 1982, I received my Bachelor's Degree in history. Mom and Daddy came to my college graduation, but not Anita. My brothers weren't physically there either. But for me, they were present.

Chapter 17:

Cancer

Daddy felt ill for after Russell died. It wasn't for awhile before he sought medical attention. He waited until I graduated college and was taking a few courses in Counseling.

I had looked through Russell's textbooks and came across the ones he had for those few classes he took on the graduate level. I read through some chapters about grief. I had experienced so much of it already.

The sadness I felt when I told Daddy I did not want to become a lawyer was still strong. But I had no choice. I had graduated college. It was time to apply to law school. I took the LSAT. I did terribly on it. But I didn't even care when I was rejected from law school. It was never my dream. It belonged to Daddy.

I could go no further with history, unable to speak or learn foreign languages fluently. My interest was European History, and in graduate school, I needed to know two European languages. I could count Italian as one. I wanted German as the second one. But even with Mom tutoring me, I could not master it.

Long ago, Stuie had self-taught himself German. But I was not Stuie, I was me. Why couldn't Stuie have lived instead of me? Why was Russell dead? He had so many dreams still that needed to happen.

That was grief talking to me. It was survivor's guilt. And I wanted to help others cope with it. I wanted to become a Counselor.

So I took a few courses in it. I feared not passing the Graduate Entrance Exam.

But now Daddy had Cancer. My life was on hold for a year. I was still married to S.

None of it mattered much.

Daddy had his bladder removed in surgery. It was too late. The Cancer had spread beyond its lining. But Daddy saw too much was unresolved. He needed more time to secure his family and put his affairs in order.

Daddy enrolled into an experimental program at Roger Williams Hospital. He became an inpatient for 9 months. He had drugs pumped into his blood through his veins.

Mom and I visited daily. She took me to lunch either at Newport Creamery or The Welcome Restaurant. Then we returned to see Daddy before I drove her home.

Daddy spent time teaching Mom about money, told her details about the CD's, the real estate holdings. He put her name on everything, including the house, and other property.

He had me drive Mom to courts across the state to vacate his bail bondsman cases.

Then he had a talk with me about my future.

"Your Mom will pay for graduate school for you. But you need to get in first."

I shared with Mom my concerns. She suggested I apply to Providence College. She remembered my freshman year there before I transferred to RIC. The staff tried to help me with my deep grief. They tried to persuade me not to marry so soon after Stuie died. She thought they would help me now.

So I applied to PC. I was advised to take two Counseling courses there first. And they assigned someone to develop strategy with me for the entrance exam.

It was discovered I had a space perception issue with hand eye coordination. It was addressed with a ruler to keep track of where the oval circles were located. I was given a left hand desk.

And miracle of miracles, I scored well enough on the entrance exam. I earned two A's in both graduate courses.

I had an acceptance letter from Providence College Graduate Counseling Program to show Daddy. It was just in time. Daddy died soon afterwards.

Chapter 18:
Rough Beginning for Robin

S got a job offer in Florida. He had gone back to school for Computer Software Engineering. His parents paid his tuition and our mortgage payments. He now graduated. And his future was in Orlando.

I went with him eventually, staying two months to finish a semester in graduate school, and to sell our small ranch.

I thought my marriage deserved one final try. With him working in his field, maybe he could be happy. Maybe the physical abuse would end. It didn't.

But something remarkable happened. I was pregnant. I needed the test to determine if the fetus would be a girl. The little girl I dreamt about, the one Stuie said I would have someday, was possibly inside me.

But a boy would be destined for decline and death. I could not, would not begin the cycle again.

S found out my check for Fotomat included small commissions. I had not told him. He decided to teach me a lesson. He kicked me on my legs repeatedly.

When he was done with my beating, I vowed it would be my last one. I needed to protect this pregnancy. I feared a miscarriage.

When he went to work on Saturday, I called my Mom to save me. She told me to drive the car to the airport. I would be helped there.

I identified myself to airport security. Many men surrounded me, took me to a room to wait. Then, they escorted me not just to the plane, but on it.

The plane was bound for Boston, the best Mom could do under the circumstances. I was afraid. I was fearful that Boston could be bad. Maybe I needed to go to the hospital faster, sooner after my beating.

As my plane soared North, I prayed for help.

The announcement was made, an emergency landing in Rhode Island was needed. But no one could leave the plane. We would resume flight onto Boston.

I began to tell passengers I had been beaten. I showed them my legs. The flight attendant ignored my pleas.

But the people I told began to make a scene. On the ground, the pilot interviewed me. He saw my legs. He declared me to be in a medical emergency. He let me off the plane.

My best friend, Rose, picked me up from airport. She took me to the hospital. The intern took pictures of my legs, but he said it was an early stage pregnancy. The fetus was intact, no harm came to it.

I decided to return to graduate school. I valued my education greatly. Daddy taught me to embrace education. He was gone, but his words still mattered to me.

The pregnancy began to be difficult. My feet got swollen, my blood pressure soared up. I had developed toxemia, as it was called then. Pre-Eclampsa is the term for it now.

I was on constant bed rest, except to eat and use the bathroom. Rose came by to keep me company. Mom worried and fussed, but in this case, there was good cause.

Then, one morning, I bled like the Red Sea. My blood filled the carpet. It looked like a murder scene. Our next door neighbor came to help in this crisis. The rescue squad rushed to save me and my unborn child.

At the hospital, Dr. Di Zoglio got ready for surgery. I

wondered whether my baby would live? Mom worried whether I would die?

Baby Robin came out of my womb from C-Section. She was tiny, obviously premature. But she kicked her attending doctor and his reward for saving her was her screaming. Dying babies don't scream. They are silent.

She was rushed off to NICU, I went into recovery. My placenta had separated. I was lucky, so was Robin.

But my estranged husband came to visit from Florida. He was the father, but he wouldn't remain my husband. We snapped a picture of the three of us. It would be the only one ever taken.

Chapter 19:
Divorce, Death, and Change

My divorce was going to take awhile, but it would happen. Mom poured money into a lawyer who would get it done. He also made sure Robin would remain safe. No visitation for the man who beat his pregnant wife. The pictures taken the day I returned to Rhode Island were proof positive of what had taken place in Orlando.

Robin got stronger, bigger, showed great progress. She came home 5 weeks after her birth. But Mom and I weren't getting alone.

Uncle Abe then died. He knew I wish to move out with Robin on my own. He told Mom before his death to use his money to buy me a washing machine.

But he had gone through his money. Mom didn't agree with my decision to leave, yet she honored Abe's wishes. She bought me the new washing machine.

I had earned my Master's Degree, but I couldn't find a job. I needed daycare hours to work. I finally went to a job fair and found a position that nearly met my requirements. It required one day with a few evening hours, the rest of the week was regular business hours.

Rose came to the rescue. She would babysit Robin. She lived above my apartment. It could be done. Mom still babysat when Robin got sick.

I lived with Robin at 588 Hartford Avenue. It was a low income neighborhood, but, at that time at least, was not dangerous. My landlord and landlady were kind to me. They helped with Robin during emergencies.

And I was dating a handsome man at that time. He took me to Italian Restaurants, bought me a pretty blue coat, gave me earrings. He, however, was not ready for marriage or fatherhood. I had to say good-bye to him. The clock was ticking away. I needed a father for my toddler. Single parenthood was not for me. I wanted a family for Robin.

Chapter 20:
David

I had met David before at the Jewish Community Center. I
saw him there again a year later. We dated briefly that first
time. He got frustrated with me. I lacked a babysitter. Mom
favored the handsome man I had dated, she wouldn't babysit
for a date with David.

When I moved out, the equation changed. I had my own place
to have David over. Robin was included in our outings. David
was obviously a family man. But would he be my husband? It
seemed not at first. He hedged at the idea of marriage. I
thought the relationship would end. It didn't. David Halpern
married me on November 26, 1988. He shook as he walked
down the aisle. His mother and sister flew in from England, a
brother flew in from Oklahoma.

Rose and David's brother had chemistry when they met. But
there was great distance involved. Rose couldn't risk it all to
move across country without a ring on her hand.

I was worried that I would no longer be the favorite daughter-
in-law. Rose Halpern was very dear to me. She loved Robin
and me. But I had my tubes tied before I married David. I
wouldn't have sick sons. It was a miracle Robin was a girl.
David was anti-abortion so that weighted heavily on my
decision not to have additional children.

David adopted Robin as a Halpern. Rose Halpern accepted
Robin as her granddaughter.

If Rose, my best friend, married the brother and had kids,

would Robin and I be tossed aside?

But it didn't happen. Truthfully, it would have wrecked our friendship. I think she knew that. My mother-in-law would have grandchildren from the brother, but he married someone else. I was more than fine with that. His wife was lovely. I went to their wedding. I felt no threat at all at this union.

Rose remarried again. There was to be peace between us. I had known Rose since age 12. Her friendship was important to me. It still is. I write this piece about this uneasy time because I wanted the truth to be told.

It was feared I liked this brother. I never did at all. But I liked the other brother in England. As David got sick after 3 years of marriage, we had visits from him while David was in the hospital. He was kind to Robin, and to me. But everything remained honorable. No wrong was committed against David. I was always faithful, although sometimes lonely.

My little girl became my companion. We traveled extensively to England, Disney World, Austria, Italy. David rarely went with us, just to England sometimes.

But , he struggled. We avoided mishaps on a double decker bus. When boarding a plane, he had a knife he used to use to open boxes at work. Somehow, he was deemed not a terrorist. He was let go.

Chapter 21:

Grandma Rose Gone

Then, a call caused us great grief. My mother-in-law had passed away. David and I went to her funeral. Her visits had been special to us. She took Robin for walks in the park, she made Swiss Steak for dinner, and a birthday cake for me. She took us for ice cream, and to dinner by the water.

She listened, she consoled, when she was there when we

needed her most the time David was first hospitalized. She stayed for a month, and we cherished every minute she was with us. I was sad to see her go. I think a part of her wanted to remain as well.

But as Daddy had often said, "Time waits for no man", so G-D took Grandma Rose home far sooner than we wanted.

My father-in-law met a lovely woman who came to live with him and his daughter and son. I met her on several trips England. She and I traveled to York together while Robin stayed in Henley. I liked her a lot. I didn't feel disloyal to Rose. While she lived, I loved her dearly. But she was gone, and life continued on.

Chapter 22:
East Side

David and I, when we were first married, lived with Robin on Hartford Avenue. Then, we moved to 14 Sargent Avenue, a much better neighborhood. We lived near my work, her school, and closer to David's job.

In a Jewish neighborhood, lots of Holocaust Survivor families resided there. I got friendly with many of them. I joined a group of Children of Holocaust Survivors. They became my extended family.

Aron Trachtenberg became a friend. He owned the textile warehouse located next to David's work. His wife, Carin, was understanding of our friendship. Aron gave me lots of advice. He had me sit with him in front at a Yom Ha Shoah Service. He spoke up for me when I needed a voice.

When he was dying, I visited him one final time at the warehouse. Carin was there. Aron never achieved remission. He knew he was doomed.

He wanted to finance me to write a book about my life. Sorry, Aron, it took so long for me to write it.

At Hebrew Day School, which Robin attended for a few years, I met the father of Robin's first crush. Michael Fink was a Professor at Rhode Island of Design. He was also a featured writer for the Rhode Island Jewish Herald. He had articles published in the Providence Journal.

He was drawn to Holocaust topics .He grew up with a child survivor. He wrote about it because he developed quite a passion for it.

I wanted him to write my Mom's story, but he insisted I do it myself. He believed in me, he pushed me beyond my comfort zone to write in a more public way than my journals I kept.

In fact, I wrote patients' social history as a social worker and later as an admissions' coordinator. Professionals who read charts often remarked that I captured who the patients were with my writing.

So I put my words out there, in these publications, and received much praise.

Alan Rosenberg published my pieces in the Short Takes Section of the Providence Journal Bulletin. Our paths would cross several times. His son would later date my daughter. And we belonged to the same temple. We would attend Saturday Services as regulars.

Many years later, he showed support for Robin and me when he attended Mom's funeral.

These two men launched me as a writer, and I will always be grateful to them.

Robin meanwhile learned technology with her first computer. It took me an entire weekend to install it. At that time, my family had a swear box. The policy was every swear earned a nickel for the box. At the end of that weekend, the box was filled with my nickels.

Thankfully, Robin mastered how to install her own computers after that first time I did it. She became my go-to person when I encountered any problems with technology. She still is.

Chapter 23:
 Anita

My sister, Anita, died unexpectedly, of a massive stroke. Mom had remarried 4 years before. So Frank became my Step-Father and Robin's Great-Grandfather. He was there with Mom and me when Anita was removed from life support. She became brain dead.

It was a horrible time. I was sick with Colitis and David's mental illness continued to progress. It was just seemingly out of the blue that Anita died.

But she had high blood pressure and hid that she did not take the prescribed pills.

Mom and Frank had to go through her stuff after she died. She had rooms full of make-up, and hidden candy in drawers. Then there was Twinkle Puffs, her surviving and beloved cat. I found a home for her.

Anita had lived with Uncle Abe and Aunt Mina after my parents threw her out for beating me. Anita had no rent to pay. Daddy owned the tenement, then Mom owned it when Daddy died. But she loved to gamble. She spent her factory pay checks on trips to Atlantic City. She even made it to Las Vegas.

Anita's money was her own to spend. Even after Abe died, Mina paid the bills. Mina's death proved tragic for Anita. There was no structure, no one to notice Anita's bad habits. Mom paid the oil bill, the podiatrist fee, anything too big for Anita to afford.

But Mom and Anita never had an easy relationship. Anita often lied to co-workers about Mom's help. And she told lies that I had moved away. There are pictures of Anita at Robin's birthday parties. I kept trying to be a good sister to her.

At the Hallmark Store one day, Anita hit Robin. I took Anita home. Mom screamed at Anita. For awhile, I stayed away from Anita.

Some years back, Anita had a friend named Felix. He was a former pharmacist because he was an alcoholic. He became a laundry attendant who Anita met doing laundry. He was a good person. His mother became friends with Anita as well. Felix tried to teach Anita to think of others in ways she hadn't except with our late brothers. He corrected her rudeness towards Mom, and me.

Sadly, Felix died. I took Anita to his funeral. When Anita brought Twinkle Puffs the Cat to the cemetery to visit his gravestone, I drove her.

I had given Anita 10 dollars for her 45th birthday. A few weeks later, she was dead. She wore the dress she was to wear to her high school reunion in her casket. Mom paid for her funeral and gravestone.

Chapter 24:
A Move to Warwick
David and I struggled at 14 Sargent Avenue to pay bills. I had been sick with Colitis, recovered, then he was getting even more mentally ill. Robin had problems at school.
Mom decided with Anita now gone, she would buy us a house in the suburbs. My former sister-in-law died and her parents wished to sell that house. It was an opportunity Mom seized upon.
But there was David himself who created an obstacle. He didn't want to go, he wished to stay in Providence. He feared change. He wanted things to stay the same.
I convinced him Robin needed a new school. He needed to do this for her. Always concerned for Robin's well being, even during his worst bouts of mental illness, he allowed the move to happen.
I made friends with Minnie Kritz when we both worked at the polls immediately after our move to Warwick. She had me visit her in her home. She was an elderly woman full of energy

and optimism.

She had also lived on the East Side of Providence before moving to Warwick. Although not from a Holocaust family like me, she was Jewish. She brought us Purim Baskets. She became a dear friend. I told her all my problems. She listened, then offered her opinion.

When Minnie got hurt one time, I called her grandson. He was suspicious of my motives. Minnie wasn't having any of that. She put him in his place. He was made to understood that I was her friend. It was odd to find out he was the former husband of my distant cousin. But it was a cousin I met perhaps once at a function.

After we moved to Warwick, we had friends that fell away. But others stuck with us. Aunt Rosalie, who we rented Sargent Avenue from, came to our parties and celebrations. She had watched Robin grow up from 4 to 11.

Cousin Cheryl let Robin into her room to play with make-up. Robin was a frequent guest there. Robin saw Rosalie and Cheryl nearly every day. Robin would rush up there to use the bathroom as David often washed his hands.

They came downstairs to our parties. And now they went across city lines to still come to our events.

My best friend, Rose, tried to put curtains up for me in my house. She finally managed to pound nails into concrete walls. I put my miniature furniture up that I inherited from Aunt Mina.

Years before, Anita and I found a hidden drawer in Mina's bureau. We found 28,000 dollars in cash. Mina had hidden the money she inherited from her friend, Albert.

Mina had lived with Albert as friends. He left her all of his money. But Mina, trapped in days of Nazi occupation of Austria, didn't trust banks.

Anita and I, per Mom, split the money. We both had bills to

pay. It was maybe the only time Anita and I shared anything in a cooperative way.

 Now, I had this house because I was the only surviving child. It was a bitter pill to swallow. I had three siblings. I hadn't been an only child. But Mom treated Robin more like a daughter than a granddaughter. Mom had Robin and me left. And she wanted to give us the world because she had lost so much of hers.

Chapter 25:
Robin's World

 Robin was a beautiful teenage. She had long, light hair, and wore size O sized jeans. She never lacked for boyfriends. I didn't always like all of them. But they mostly came and went, except for maybe 3.

I didn't know everything about her any more. She had never kept secrets from me while she was a child. But she was a teenager now, searching for more independence from me.

I didn't see the signs at first anything was wrong. 911 had happened. We as a country were on edge. So I missed the symptoms.

But her private school told me all was not well with Robin. The pediatrician realized there was a problem.

Robin was hospitalized. There were stories of that time that only Robin can tell. I had to cope, make changes, for Robin to resume her life. Robin needed a new school. I got her one, across town, with a school waiver. I had to drive her daily. I no longer could work. I now had Asthma.

Robin began to blossom again. She made plans for her future. I aided her in achieving them with visits to Savannah. She wanted to go to an art school down South. I was willing to let go, and Mom was willing to pay.

But we didn't see Savannah for more than a beautiful tourist city. We did teatime in quaint places, rode down the Savannah River on a boat, we shopped along the shore, we dined at the Olde Pink House. Robin and I sure had fun in Savannah.

Well, except once when I exited a taxi and my door slightly touched a parked car. The occupants surrounded me, making clear their intentions to do me harm. Robin rushed into the Sheraton, and returned with security. I was released unharmed. The occupants were told to go on their way. No police were called. This was the Southern way to handle the matter.

Robin did 7 weeks at SCAD. She begged to come home. I hesitated at first. I wanted Robin to give that college more time to work out.

David, always a loyal father, took the flight with me. He couldn't help much, but he wanted to give support to his Bobbit.

In reality, Robin represented much in my relationship with David. He choose her as his daughter. I selected David as her father. I never had a doubt he would be a good Dad, and he was. He taught her how to play chess while he was hospitalized. He took her treat and treating during our Sargent Avenue days. He brought her to the Rochambeau Library, to CVS. He worked hard to provide for her in a job that was hard on him.

Even as he declined, he always thought of his little girl.

Chapter 26:
David Slips Away

David started out taking me out to nice restaurants for breaking the fast for Yom Kippur. We celebrated anniversaries in New York, Montreal, and the Von Trapp Lodge in Vermont. But he slipped away from me.

We had Robin. We raised her together. We gave her our love and values we shared.

David's father had been Jewish, his mother was not. David converted after 5 years of marriage, to become, as Robin said, a whole Jew, instead of half of one.

David kept the Passover, fasted on Yom Kippur, prayed in and out of synagogue with a prayer book. He practiced what he preached. He never swore at me, was faithful, a hard worker. We discussed what was best for Robin, we nearly always agreed.

But David, although he co-parented with me, often worshiped with me, became and remains my friend. I became his care provider. He could no longer work. He had appointments to go to, I took him.

But my Asthma was very serious. I was in ICU so many times. Robin saved me many of those times. Second hand smoke was killing me. David's pipe was the cause. He couldn't quit. He tried.

I held onto him. I wanted to be a good wife. We saw Dr. Martin, a friendly psychiatrist, until David's insurance changed. We went to family counseling. We saw social workers. David's medication was changed, adjusted, modified. He was hospitalized. I prayed, I cried, I begged G-D to help.

But I was dying.

Chapter 27:

Scott

Robin came back home, not just to David and me, but to her steady boyfriend. Robin went to live with him and his family so she could study in Boston.

She returned home, with her boyfriend in tow. I didn't mind at all. At least, my little bird was home. She got pregnant, I welcomed the news, but also feared it because of what happened to both my brothers.

Mom paid for expensive testing. There was a second test I didn't have while pregnant with Robin. And all testing was now available in Rhode Island.

Robin was having a healthy boy! It was a miracle.

Mom now suffered from Alzheimer's Disease. She had lost so many. But this great-grandson was a special gift to her. She was overjoyed.

And Scott came into the world, as a full term baby. I was there in the labor room when he arrived. His parents let me name him Scott in memory of Stuie. Stuie's middle name had been Scott.

They lived with David and me. Life seemed great. David embraced his role as grandfather as fully as his condition permitted. I gave up my study so Scott had his own bedroom. Family and friends bought gifts, a rocking chair, a swing, a crib. I got him a cute hamper, a changing table.

Robin read, "Good Night, Moon", to him. She loved her son. She was so proud of him. He was very well behaved. Robin and I took him to a modeling agency. They agreed he was handsome, but perhaps too tall at that time.

Chapter 28:

David Leaves, T. Enters

 But my Asthma was nearly done with me. A very serious close call I had. Robin feared my death. The house had to be sold. I couldn't manage financially anymore. And David had to go.

 I put him in a motel, at first, then got him an apartment. I still took him on his appointments, I paid his bills. I didn't act separated from him, we kept the joint bank accounts.

 Robin, Scott's father, Scott, and I moved to the Regency Apartments. I paid for a wedding, their honeymoon, too. But all was not well.

 Robin had her family now. She didn't want any interference from me. I had to go into my own apartment, letting this young family be on their own.

I still visited and babysat Scott.

 I lived alone at the Villa Del Rio. I now had a legal divorce from David. It was a friendly divorce, and it still is. But I was only 48. Too young to just be alone. So Robin set up my computer and put me on Jdate, on my request.

 There I found T. T was the guy from Long Island. He progressed to a steady conversation, and moved on to coming to see me. But he almost changed his mind. He secretly did not like the sound of my voice when he called me on the phone.

 He came anyhow, but with the stipulation that he gave me the first five minutes to prove I was who I said I was.

 He went off the wrong exit, for reasons I learned later. I had to go find him in a mall parking lot. I saw him wave me down. I knew it was him. I got out of the car to greet him.

 Fireworks are only suppose to happen in a movie. But honestly, I saw fireworks when I looked at T. Maybe he did, too, because he kissed me. I didn't push him away. Maybe I should have. The instant chemistry I felt could not be denied.

When I met S as a very young woman, I never felt this intense passion. I might have felt some with a boyfriend I had for a year. I never felt it for David. I had a deep friendship, mutual respect, common values for him. That is suppose to add up to romantic love, but it never did.

Here was this man, a stranger really, and I felt that extreme passion immediately. Needless to say, romance happened very shortly thereafter.

And it stayed for awhile. For two years, we kept up our relationship. He came to Rhode Island, I went to Long Island. We seemed inseparable.

I went with him on business, I saw the condition of his house. He went with my grandson and me for ice cream. He came to a friend's Bat Mitzvah with me, attended Rosh Hashanah at my temple.

He is Jewish so he understood me. He respected my Mom greatly. Even to this day, since her death, he speaks highly of her. He let me talk about the Holocaust. He wanted to learn more.

Then my daughter and grandson moved to Florida. That left a big void in my life, one that T proposed to fill with my move to Long Island.

Mom and my Step-Father lived in assisted living. So I would come weekly, maybe staying over sometimes, at first, in a hotel, then doing a round trip in one day.

T suggested we winter in Florida. So I rented an apartment down there. He came sometimes, not staying the whole season. I spent time with my family.
He called less.

Then I developed pneumonia. I was seriously ill. I asked T to come drive me home to Long Island, or just let me die. He decided to rescue me. He brought me back up North, and my regular Asthma doctor got me better.

I returned to Florida the following winter. I needed to come North again because I had interfered with my daughter one time too many. He flew out, we drove back.

I found out soon enough T had dated a few women while I had been in Florida. I don't know that I forgave him. I never forgot it. But we moved on from it. I still thought he loved me. He cared enough at least to save my life. That had to count for something.

T and I went on some great trips. Las Vegas and Hawaii were two places we went together. He had always dreamt of visiting Hawaii. I had been there once as a child with Mom and Uncle Abe.

So off we went, first to Los Angeles, to change planes. It was onto Hawaii, 5 more hours to fly.

T and I climbed Diamond Head. He was disappointed we didn't quite reach the top. But it was a beautiful view just the same. We witnessed someone air lifted off the top. Someone had a heart attack. I was glad we hadn't done it.

T and I dined out. We walked around Waikiki, taking in what it had to offer. It was an expensive place to shop and eat, but T was generous.

Pearl Harbor held great meaning. We saw the sunken ship's remains. We were moved to hear men who survived the attack on that fateful day choose to have their ashes join their fallen friends who perished from the Japanese ambush.

That segment of the trip was fine. The Disneyland portion was a disaster. We met a Facebook friend there.

T wanted to ride wild rides. My friend did, too. So off they went without me. My friend rode in separate cars from T, so I don't blame her. She did not flirt with him.

But I felt he was inconsiderate to leave me alone.

Las Vegas, for me, for the best time I had with T. We did not gamble or drink. We went to see Hoover Dam, to walk from Nevada to Arizona, in two different time zones. Best of all, I bought Sophie the Purple Unicorn at the gift shop.

We rode on the Grand Canal at the Venetian. We dined Italian. We strolled along the shops at this magnificent hotel. Our suite is what people dream about, but we lived it.

There were other trips we took. We went to a wedding in Arizona and visited my Cousin Gayle while there. We drove to San Diego from Phoenix. We were shocked at the security detail near Yuma. We weren't trying to cross into Mexico, yet we were questioned why we were there at all.

San Diego itself was nice. We stayed at a W Hotel. Its design was unique, chic, and modern. We walked far, ate much, and even shopped at Macy's. Best of all, we saw the Pandas at the zoo. It was a fun couple's trip.

T and I went to Montreal and stayed at the Queen Elizabeth, an old grand hotel, in the center of town.

He came with me to the old Sephardic Jewish Cemetery, and to the Holocaust Museum.

We took two cruises together. We dined at elegant establishments. We went to the Jacuzzi. We sat on the balcony, to see the ship depart from shore.

These trips, and the others I haven't highlighted here, were part of why I liked being with T. He enjoyed travel, as I did, and still do. It was something we had in common. It was our time together to explore.

Chapter 29:

Mom

Mom was a Holocaust Survivor, then she endured new
hardships . But she still enjoyed life when others would have
despair.

Mom's reward was towards the end of her life when she had a
Great-Grandson to love. Because Scott did not have Muscular
Dystrophy, she got to see him run, climb, and do everything
little boys do when they are healthy.

Mom had sold the house she loved in Garden City. She was
too confused to manage and my Step-Father, Frank, was too
physically frail. So they went to West Bay Manor, an assisted
living residence

It was there Scott came to see them with either his mother or
me. Scott's presence gave them such joy. He brought light into
their basement level apartment. When there was a party, they
wanted Scott there. His youth took away the depressing things
that elderly people must accept.

Scott and his Mom moved away to Florida, but that did not
end Scott's visits with his Great-Grandmother . When Scott
was up North visiting his father, I was allowed to bring him to
see Mom.

Frank had since died, and Mom was now at Tamarisk, in the
Renaissance Unit.

One time, Scott and I brought a birthday cake as a belated
celebration for his May birthday. Mom had a poor appetite by
this time, but she tried to eat a little. She was thrilled she had
this time with him.

Mom forgot many details, but she always knew who Scott
was, how old he was, where he lived. Scott had the patience to
put up with her confusion about everything else.

Mom's condition declined by October of 2012. Hospice
needed to be involved with her care. T and I drove from Long

Island to Warwick, Rhode Island, after Storm Sandy, to deliver papers required for Hospice care to start. Mail service had not become fully restored.

I was told Mom had 6 final months to live. So I came often to see her. I kept my daughter informed of her grandmother's worsening situation.

In April of 2013, I got the call Mom probably had a very short time left. I packed my funeral dress , then drove along Route 95, along the Connecticut coastline, into Rhode Island.

A few months before, I bought that dress at Macy's at the Walt Whitman Mall. I didn't want a repeat of when I bought my funeral dress for my sister's funeral in 1995. I was numb, and my best friend, Rose, had to really push me to make a purchase.

This time, I was preparing for the inevitable, but was not yet in full grief mode. I decided an all black dress was not for me to wear. Mom hated black. She was a cheerful woman who liked bright colors. I would honor her life, not mourn her death, by wearing a dress with both black and blue in it. It had a matching blue sweater that went with it.

Hospice staff were with me to guide me through Mom's active dying because Mom had been moved to a nursing home in that last month. It was not my wish, but Tamarisk was not licensed to provide that end- of- life care Mom required.

I sat with my Mom, remembering a conversation she had with me a few weeks before. In a moment of clarity, Mom asked me if I would be okay after she passed away? I promised her I would be. I am not sure I told the total truth, but I said it anyhow because Mom needed to feel free to let go.

I had to help Mom transition to the next phase. But Mom was anxious. She was struggling to take this final step. So Hospice gave her medication to let her drift away peacefully.

The next day was her last one in this world. As a former

geriatric Social Worker, I knew that even a patient in a coma can often still hear what is spoken. I told her heaven was a beautiful place. That everyone in our family, except Robin, Scott, and me, were waiting for her. I gave her my permission for her to could go to them now.

The sun was going down, and as it did, a shadow past over the portrait of Mom that hung on the wall. An artist, also interned with her at Fort Ontario, had painted that picture of Tina Korner when she was 23.

But now as the shadow cast darkness over the painting, Mom began to breathe heavily. I saw the muscles in her neck strain, then there was no movement at all. Mom was dead.

Mom was gone, and my cell phone stopped working. My cell phone was new to me, and I didn't know when to charge it before it was out of energy. I had to rush outside, into my car, to charge it so I could tell Robin her Grandmother had just died.

But more than that, I have to arrange for Robin and Scott's flight for the funeral. Of course, they wanted to be there for that farewell, and I needed them to be with me.

Scott was 6 at the time, old enough to be able to preserve memory of Great-Bubbe. I was grateful for those 6 years he had her in his life. I was satisfied that somehow I gave Mom a granddaughter and Robin gifted her with a great-grandson.

Her granddaughter and great-grandson did not replace the three children she had to bury, but they were new generation who existed because she survived the Holocaust.

Mom planted 4 seeds when she had children. Sadly, 3 of them did not endure long enough. I did, and I was able to have a daughter. A small branch, but still hope for the future. Then Robin had Scott. The branch extended slightly. We have yet to know if Scott extends the branch further into the future. But there is that possibility that he will.

So that gave me the strength to keep going after Mom died.

I bought Scott a suit to wear to Mom's funeral. He looked solemn and dignified in it. I snapped a picture of him wearing it to record that day for him, and for me.

The three of us stood over Mom's grave, then, as per Jewish custom, we each threw shovels full of dirt over it. Mom's casket could no longer been seen as the few other mourners did the same.

Mom was seemingly gone for good. But she wasn't.

Chapter 30:

Holocaust Memories

Mom never wanted me to go to Poland, where her extended family were exterminated in a death camp. I wished to go anyhow, but during her lifetime, I never had the opportunity to do so.

At first, Poland was locked behind the Iron Curtain. I would never have considered traveling to a Communist Country. Jews were often mistreated under Communism, and I doubted Jewish visitors fared well.

But then the curtain was parted in 1989, and Poland became possible for me. However, I could not go on my own, like I had in Western and Central Europe. My limited knowledge of German, Italian, and French were enough to help me navigate in Paris, Vienna, Zurich, Genoa, Berlin, and Munich.

I even ventured to Prague and Budapest. Prague was a pleasure, with friendly Czechs to aid me, Budapest was a hardship, with anti-Semitism ever present.

With my move to Long Island in 2010. I was put into a new position to develop a relationship with Andrea. She is a Second Generation, like me. Her father was a survivor. She is on the Board of Directors of the Glen Cove Holocaust Memorial and Tolerance Center. She is also someone who knows how to get things done. She doesn't know the meaning of the words can't, won't, or impossible. Her vocabulary includes words like, determination, persistence, networking, persuasion, investigating, hard work, and success!

She decided she would organize a trip for the March of the Living for the Long Island vicinity. I had told her of my desire to visit Treblinka, and she created an opportunity for me to fulfill that wish.

And so in April of 2014, I flew on El Al with Andrea and her group to Poland. Andrea had arranged for our chartered bus, 2 guides, and a security guard, to keep us safe, and to provide structure. I never felt afraid. Andrea made sure none of us did.

Treblinka was an experience I will never forget as long as I live. I felt the presence of not just my extended family, but the spirits of all who were slaughtered there.

I left slips of papers with my family's names on the gravestone marked Austria: William, Regina, Jakob, Moishe, Hershel, and especially Esther Kudish.

My family were among the 900,000 Jews who came off trains, separated, shaved, stripped, gassed, burned to ash, then either scattered to the winds, buried in a mass pit, or dumped to the bottom of lakes.

The camp was largely torn down, but traces of it have been rediscovered by archaeologists, and a more accurate description of its layout is now known.

The Jews were sent into a building where a Star of David was engraved into the front. But they learned rather quickly that the space they were crowded into was not sacred at all, but a place they were to die.

After they were lifeless, naked, piled up as corpses, they were dragged out to the pit where they were set on fire. Their belongings were to be used by people the Germans deemed worthy of life. The Jews were seen by the Nazis and their collaborators, including Ukrainians, Poles, Austrians, among many others, as a burden to be eliminated. But in fact, the killers were the monsters.

But there were a few pleasant moments for me during this once-in-a life time trip. I spotted pastry shop in Krakow, enjoying my European torte, layered with chocolate and whipped cream.

I made lifetime friends with Anna and Asher, as well as Donna. Anna and Asher's daughter, Miriam, would later prove to be a very good friend to me.

I would in the future attend Donna's adult Bat Mitzvah. Donna, had, in fact, said the Kaddish for my family in Treblinka. For me, Donna added a holiness to a very sacred few minutes I had to mourn my family properly.

Andrea granted me a life experience that never could have happened without her intervention. And I know Andrea will continue to create this opportunity for others to go on The March of the Living. Since this trip I took in 2014, she has led yet another group in 2016. She has planned one for 2018 as well.

I have been truly blessed to have been befriended by Andrea. But sadly, that golden chapter I enjoyed on Long Island would come to an end.

Chapter 31:
 Long Island

 I came home from Poland and flew into JFK, from where T
picked me up. I knew immediately that he took the time I was
away to talk to other women on line, on dating sites which he
paid for, from the small rent money I gave him each month.
 I had confronted him many times after checking his cell
phone for proof. He finally stopped denying the truth, stating I
had too many problems. I had Asthma, I had spent too much
money, I couldn't help him any longer doing laundry.
 I resisted leaving for far too long. Not because I loved him, I
no longer did. I had loved him greatly. But his actions caused
me to lose those feelings for him. What I did still love was
Long Island, and I didn't want to leave it.
 Long Island gave me Fire Island to walk along in the summer.
I saw the lighthouse after a stroll from Robert Moses Beach,
Field 5. I walked further on, to Kismet.
I admired the beautiful summer homes that lined the narrow
lanes, where tricycle carried groceries, because cars were
rarely used. I ate ice cream by the ferry dock, where I saw
people disembark off the boat. Sometimes, I ventured further
out to Saltaire, Fair Harbor, even Altantique. The breeze blew
gently from the seashore and above flew planes from Mac
Arthur Airport in Islip.
 It was from Mac Arthur I flew to Florida to see Robin and
Scott. It is a cute airport where TSA agents knew me well, as I
used it every few months to be in Florida for birthdays,
science fairs, anniversaries.
 On Long Island, I discovered Brieremere Pies in Riverhead. I

loved their chocolate cream pie the best. In earlier days, T took me out there. I ended up going there myself in later years.

But most of all, I had my synagogue, Temple Beth-El. It was my sanctuary, my place to worship, to mourn my family, to celebrate the Torah, to sit under a Sukkah. I also had my temple family.There were many of them, but I must mention Amy Pater Podhurst and Dr. Howard Schneider in particular.They knew me, heard my family stories, sat with me at Sisterhood Luncheons, Yom Ha Shoah Services, to remember the Holocaust, at a Sousa Mendes Supper to recall a righteous Portuguese man who saved Jews during the Holocaust in France.

Rabbi Jeff Clopper and Cantor Allison Levine, whom I name with fondness, led us in prayer, gave us issues to reflect upon, and offered me the level of spirituality I sought.

I loved my temple dearly, and to leave it took much time and courage on my part.

Chapter 32:
Near Death In The Air, Happiness at Sea

In August of 2016, I was flying to Florida to join Robin and Scott on a cruise in the Carribean on the Oasis of the Seas.

But with Southwest, one must check into the flight 24 hours before. I had my computer ready to do so. I was well seasoned from many trips before how to do it. Yet, the computer blocked me. My Smartphone wouldn't permit me to do it. It was finally T who found a way for me to do what I should have done easily.

Off I went on the plane, ascending up from Islip, when a bird got sucked into the engine. Since I sat at the wing, I saw it happen.

I knew all was not well. We didn't follow the flight pattern I knew. We kept circling Fire Island, where I saw a US Coast Guard Ship below us. The Captain told of what had happened. He awaited instructions from the makers of the plane what to do next.

When the crew learned what to do, they shared it with the passengers. We were to fly low, along land, to Baltimore, Maryland, to make an emergency landing. They were prepared to deal with crash landings. La Guardia and Kennedy were busy airports that could not accommodate what we needed, for all planes to be halted, the runway closed to other flights, and the airport to be mostly empty.

As we flew, I sat alone in my row, fearful this was to be my final moments alive. But I felt Mom's spirit on one side of me, Daddy's ghost on the other side. I heard them both say they would protect me, I would not die.

I thought of when Robin had Cancer, and I prayed Mom would protect my little bird from dying. Robin lived! I remembered other times, too, when I collapsed on the feet of a security guard at doors of Huntington Hospital, and he gave me CPR. I recalled how my friend, Art Abrams, had stopped me from going to Mac Arthur Airport on icy morning roads by telling me the flight was cancelled.

I had to believe my parents' souls reached out to me that day in that sky, as we landed safely in Baltimore.

Another plane was dispatched to take the passengers onto

Orlando. We received vouchers for a future flight from Southwest.

I went on that cruise with Robin and Scott where we landed in ports of St. Martin, Puerto Rico, and Haiti. Scott and I shared a cabin. We feasted on afternoon pastry on our balcony. We got pizza, had ice cream, did fine dining. We watched a play from Broadway.

I had the time of my life because my life was spared. I didn't die over Fire Island, a place I loved so much.

Chapter 33:
Relationship with T and Leaving Long Island

When is it a enough to leave a 9 year relationship? I don't really know the answer. The house I lived in with T had been horrible for years. I got a nail in my arm from holding onto the banister, carrying wash into the dark, moldy basement. I tried to clean the mold off the bathroom ceiling with Tilex. It always came back anyhow. The yard was littered with trailers, or had grass taller than I was. We no longer had a stove. I had to park on the grass in front, the driveway had many vehicles T used to do recycling.

I had enjoying going to Brooklyn with him, when he got paid for the bottles he collected. He often took me for pastry and take-out on the way back. But he began to take me less and less.

I loved the trips we took together, from California to Canada, Florida to Maine; Savannah was special, but Las Vegas and

Hawaii were my favorite trips.

T had made sure I ate, he gave me money so I would. We survived Storm Sandy together. He took me to the hospital when I needed to go.

But T became cruel. He never hit me, not even once. He never forced himself on me against my will. He did put me down, make fun of me, belittle me, stopped spending time with me, told me no one else would want me. And in the end, he screamed at me for little things. He never threatened me, but told me that there was the front door, use it, if I wished.

And so one day, I did.

I don't know what my breaking point was because I was numb by that time. Just on a whim, I finally decided to go. I was afraid to leave because of many reasons of health and finances. But one day, I made the decision to go.

I just went. I didn't leave Long Island immediately. I was broke, with no resources to go anywhere. But what I did have was a community of friends in Huntington, in Greater Long Island, and beyond.

Facebook, with its sites, afforded me the network of friends I had. In addition, Facebook helped me to reconnect with people from my past, old friends, high school classmates, others who shared my family's Holocaust roots, still more who worshiped at my temple.

And I had Andrea to help me as well.

With everyone's cooperation, I had places to stay while I sorted out what to do next. Asher and Anna's daughter, Miriam, was one of the people who opened up her home to me. She listened to my concerns. She offered me to stay longer, if need be.

I had to have money to go somewhere else. My network of friends, and friends of friends, reached out to me, and provided for me financially. Art Abrams again offered good information. He suggested I use the Autotrain.

My cousin, Michelle, allowed me to stay with her, on route to Virginia. She, her husband, and two sons made me feel welcomed in their home. We caught up on old family stories. She even showed me a picture of my Mom at her wedding, years ago.

Michelle lives close to the Maryland border. When I crossed it, I felt a sense of loss. I was of the North, and I was leaving the region of the country that had always been my home. I was going South, to a section of the country visited by me, but was never where I believed I could ever belong.

Chapter 34:
A New Beginning

I had to begin again, at age 57, and I was terrified.

The Autotrain pulled slowly out of its Lorton Station at first, then gained speed. I tried not to think too hard about my future. Nothing could be done until I reached Sanford Station, in Florida.

My daughter and grandson lived in Central Florida. It was natural that I would relocate there. But I had tried to live there before, and I failed a few times.

I now had only the resources my friends had given me. I had no address to call my own, only a week's stay at a hotel. My Hashimoto's Disease seemed worse. My nerves were shot.

But Robin organized our search for a place for me to live within my means. And Scott kept my morale up when I was feeling low.

Robin found a listing on Craig's List in Winter Park. We went there together, and we both agreed that if I was accepted as a tenant, I had found my new home.

It was in a fabulous neighborhood, solidly middle class homes on one part of the street, wealthy houses on the other side. There was a park nearby, and the Winter Park Hospital not very far away.

I had left my furniture up North so I needed a new bed, a bureau, a nightstand, kitchen table and chairs, and a place for Scott to sleep during overnight visits.

Art Abrams suggested Ikea as a furniture store with affordable prices. Scott accompanied me there. I was a nervous wreck so Scott took care of details on my behalf.

I picked out pretty blue furniture. T had all brown furniture left over from his parents that I never liked. I wanted light colors to reflect my new life in the Sunshine State.

Scott helped me move from belongings from the hotel, into my car, then to my new home. Robin went shopping with me for essentials like a shower curtain, garbage can, linens for the bed, a few pieces of cheap china.

The deliveries began to arrive. I started to have some order added to my still chaotic life.

There was dealings with the DMV to obtain a Florida driver's license and to register my car, the bureaucracy of having my old banking account closed with a new one in Florida opened, notifying companies of my new address, getting onto an insurance carrier for Florida, and having new doctors to fill my prescriptions.

Then I had a new crisis to deal with. A routine check -up at a new dentist revealed a growth in my mouth that needed to be removed immediately. I had to pay for it because the dentist I had was out-of-network. But I felt the lump in my mouth, and decided I had to act.

I joined a Reform Temple. I needed that spirituality returned to me. Scott became my Friday night fellow worshiper.

I had left my tricycle behind on Long Island, and I missed it terribly. Back on Long Island, T and I rode in Caumsett Park, especially after my Mom died. In Rhode Island, I loved my bike as a child, riding to Garden City to escape my troubles.

So Scott found me one online and ordered it for me. It arrived, placed in the back, per Scott's instructions to Fed Ex. My then neighbors, Troy and Nicole, assembled it for me as a surprise to cheer me up.

I went on dating sites, only to stumble badly. One guy offered me a massage. Scott blocked and deleted him, on my request. There was one other I thought was a nice guy. We chatted sometimes, but our conversations never got too far. We seemed to have little in common. I doubted there really was a connection between us. I still held out hope that meeting him in person would be a positive thing.

Chapter 35:

Saying Good-Bye

Meanwhile, I received sad news that my cousin, Cheryl, had passed away suddenly. I was at a mall when I learned of her death. I decided immediately that I was to attend her funeral.

On Sargent Avenue, many years ago, my family lived beneath my aunt, uncle, and cousin. Cheryl would take little Robin upstairs, into her room, to do her nails a pretty pink. She showed Robin her fashion magazines. She liked having Robin around, and Robin enjoyed being there, upstairs, away from her father constant washing his hands.

Now Cheryl had died, and I lived so far away. I redeemed points I accumulated from my frequent visits to Florida to visit Robin and Scott. I booked my flight, my hotel, and rental car.

Scott kept me company the next day. He helped me get a bike lock to secure it for when I was gone. We selected a travel bag as a carry on. I organized my clothes before Scott and I attended Friday night services.

Next morning, I dropped Scott off at home to my daughter. I got Map Quest to find me a route to the airport without tolls. I had arranged with my on-line potential suitor to meet me at the airport. He worked there.

But all did not go well in that brief encounter. As nice as he was, there was no chemistry whatsoever between us. I had been too hasty in deciding to start online dating sites at this point in time.

I fled into the TSA-Pre line, to escape what I never should have begun at all. I got breakfast to calm me down. Then, it was time to board the plane.

As the plane landed in Warwick, Rhode Island, I realized no one would be waiting for me on the other end. Except T did call me to see if I landed safely. I was honestly grateful for his call. I had not ended communications with him. Not because I would ever go back to that dangerous house with mold and a backyard full of hoarded trailers. I wouldn't. But having someone I had in my life for 9 years requires time for closure. I still didn't have closure yet.

After I secured my rental car, checked into my hotel, I headed off to Pawtucket, to see someone also from my past. My former second husband, David, lived there. I had arranged to pick him up, and for us to go to Gregg's Restaurant.

But he was nervous from the start. We drove beyond his comfort zone. He smoked outside the restaurant before we were seated. He ordered and ate his food. I enjoyed my order of Tuna Fish Sandwich with Sweet Potato Fries. We had delicious rolls and pickles, too.

He was on edge so I ordered dessert to go. I realized I needed to check into my Southwest flight because it was 24 hours prior to my return home. Something went wrong. David had no concept of what I was attempting to do. He does not live in the world of cell phones and computers.

To relieve him of any further confusion, I drove him back home. I left it to Robin to figure out what went wrong with the confirmation of the flight process.

I returned to my hotel. I got comfortable in bed and watched my favorite cooking shows. I fell asleep with my television on, like I used to when I lived with T.

I awoke the next day, showered, and dressed for Cheryl's funeral. My hotel was located very close to both the airport and the Jewish cemetery. So I did not have far to drive.

When I picked up my rental car, I was given a brand new

2018 Toyota Camry. It felt very comfortable, safe, and reliable. It was also black. It looked very respectable for what I was about to use it for.

I drove to Lincoln Park Cemetery, to the chapel where Cheryl's light colored casket now was. I had a flashback to when my sister's funeral was held here in 1995. I sat in front with my Mom as we mourned together.

I walked up to my Cousin Gayle, Cheryl's sister, and hugged her. Last time I saw her was in Arizona, when T and I visited her and her husband, Jerry, in their lovely home. Gayle fed us delicious food. Jerry showed T what he stored in the garage. That was a happy visit. This was not.

The funeral began with Rabbi Adler presiding. He spoke prayers from our Jewish tradition. He then offered the podium to Gayle, who spoke from her heart. Cheryl had cared for others, even though she required much assistance as well. Cheryl had been a beauty in her youth, she sold Avon to help others be more beautiful, too. Cheryl loved to sing. She knew how to coordinate her clothes to the latest fashion trends.

It was then time for the hearse to take Cheryl to her final resting place with her both parents. We followed in our cars. Her casket was lowered into the ground. It is Jewish custom for mourners to put shovels full of dirt on top. Gayle and Jerry went first to perform this sad task. Then a devoted friend of Cheryl's went next. I went after he finished. I did a sloppy job, as my tears began.

But I was truly glad I came. I owed it to my cousin to be there at her funeral. She had been kind to my child when Robin needed some special attention.

I did not have to go far to visit my immediate family's graves. The Chernick headstone had been visible from where Cheryl was buried. I saw Russell's gravestone enclosure with his picture inside was loose. I had struggled for a year to get

Stuie's enclosure reattached and spent money I didn't really have to pay for it. I knew I had neither the money or time to do anything at all. In fact, I realized that since I lived so far away, all the enclosures would eventually be compromised. Daddy no longer had an American flag in place in front of his grave. The last one I had placed before I moved away to Florida. I would not be there and so could not put a new one in.

I felt ashamed at first. Mom had kept up the gravestones. Even Frank had helped her to do it. But Mom was here, among my family, in this plot. At least her Holocaust Survivor's emblem was still attached to her gravestone.

I got on the cold ground to hug each gravestone, of Mom's, Daddy's, Stuie's, Russell's, even Anita's. I cried I wouldn't be back for a long time.

Suddenly, the sun came out from beneath a cloud. I got up to my feet, turned around, got in my car, and went to the reception being held after the burial. There was good food offered by a view of Narragansett Bay. Gayle and I spoke of old times, good and bad. Then we both stated that Rhode Island was part of our past, not our future.

I drove past my former home on Narragansett Parkway on the way to the airport. So many memories were there. It had been my home with Robin and David for 11 years. Scott spent his first year of life there. But, it had a few different owners since I sold it in 2007.

My flight was delayed for 3 hours so I grabbed a bite to eat at Johnny Rocket. I settled into the waiting area. I fell asleep briefly then woke up. Some people had texted me, including T.

I boarded my flight finally. I left Rhode Island in the pitch black. I could see nothing of what I was leaving behind. But I did see the lights of the Florida coastline as I approached it.

Mom always left darkness behind. I am trying, too.

Miscellaneous Essays:
Essay 1:

It was school vacation. I asked my Mom whether I could resume more responsibility with Stuie by taking him on the Cranston Transvan to both Garden City and the Warwick Mall?

Mom said yes. She knew how much I loved my little brother. I would help him and protect him to the very best of my ability.

So the Transvan arrived to take us to Garden City. The driver used the wheelchair lift with confidence as Mom observed for herself. Stuie was in good hands.

The ride didn't take too long. But Stuie and I were excited to be on this adventure together. We took this time to plan our visit. We were only allotted 3 hours before the van returned for us.

We decided lunch was first. We went to Newport Creamery. I carefully looked two ways twice before I pushed Stuie's Orange wheelchair across the busy road.

We made it without incident. Someone opened the heavy glass door for us, and I pushed the wheelchair over the slight hump no one else would take notice of.

We took our place at a booth. At least I did. Stuie had to remain seated in his wheelchair at the end. I was strictly instructed by both our parents that I could not attempt to lift him out of it.

The waitress was cheerful. She took our orders without making any out- of- the- ordinary remarks about Stuie being in a wheelchair at such a young age.

We drank our tall glasses of coffee milk first, then came the hot dogs with fries. Stuie needed assistance with cutting his food and having his plate placed closer to him. But this was second nature to me. I was taught from a young age to do for both boys what they could no longer do for themselves.

Of course, we had hot fudge sundaes for dessert. We made a mess for the waitress to clean up. But she seemed patient with us. There was no scolding from her, only smiling.

With our meal eaten, it was off to Woolworths. Again, we had to cross a busy street. But when cars saw the wheelchair in the crosswalk, they stopped immediately for us.

Inside Woolworth, we went down all the aisles. The store detective followed us around, but we didn't mind. In fact, when something was too high up on the shelf, the man reached it for us.

Time flew by, it was time to meet the van. The driver was already there. He saw us approach so he got the wheelchair lift down, ready for use. Stuie bravely endured being placed on it with his wheelchair, and listened to the grinding noise the lift made as he got closer to the level of the van itself.

We made it home safe and sound. Mom was there to greet us. She asked us if we had a good time, what we ate, did we enjoy our lunch?

The next day, the van came for us again, this time to take us to Warwick Mall. There would be no streets to cross once we entered its doors. It was mainly on one floor, unless we took the elevator in the two anchor stores. We never bothered to do that. It wasted time. Again, we only had three hours to be here.

We again ate first, and it was also at Newport Creamery. We followed our same routine. We ordered the same food, but we enjoyed it greatly.

It was off to the shops. There was a blue shirt with a colorful trolley car on it. I really wanted it, but I didn't have enough money to buy it. But Stuie did. He bought me that shirt with no expectation of repayment.

He simply said, "Ella, I want you to have this gift from me."

Only Stuie called me Ella. Because he thought of me as being Cinderella. Ella was for short.

So we returned home, and I showed Mom what Stuie bought me. She hugged Stuie, "You are a good brother!"

Stuie nodded, "Because I have a wonderful sister who doesn't leave me home alone."

It took much effort now to go places with Stuie. He had a hunched posture in his wheelchair. He had to be repositioned often. He had difficulty using any muscles in his hands.

My older brother, Russell, who also had Duchenne Muscular Dystrophy, and in a wheelchair, was not as hunched over.

Passover came the next day. Uncle Abe came over to lead our Seder. But he stole glances at Stuie and whispered words I couldn't hear to Mom. Mom seemed to turn away from her brother.

Stuie drank some grape wine offered to him. He must have drank too much because he fell under the table. Daddy and Uncle Abe lifted him off the floor. Not only was he not hurt, he was laughing.

A few weeks later, Stuie laid dead in his coffin. I don't want him to be dead, so I write about him.

Essay 2:

It was the first vacation little Stuie was allowed to take with us. The year before, my older brother and I went to Atlantic City with Mom and Uncle Abe. This year, it was just a visit to Cape Cod. We stayed at the Dennis Hotel in Falmouth with Mom and Uncle Abe.

Stuie and I were inseparable. We did everything together. We liked the same foods, and enjoyed doing the same things. And so we headed to the beach with our sand buckets.

Ar first, we stayed on the sand. But the sun got hot so we got into the water. We didn't go too far at all. I thought we would be okay. But a tide came in and pulled Stuie away from the show. I tried at first to reach him, but water got in my mouth. I had to cough it out.

So I did what I thought would help. I screamed that Stuie was drowning. A middle aged woman answered the call for help. She leaped in and grabbed Stuie in time. She pulled us both to shore.

Then Mom and Uncle Abe came running with medical assistance. Stuie was checked. He was okay, if not shaken. But he was taken away for further evaluation, just to be sure.

I was upset at myself. It had been all my fault. If Stuie had drowned, I would have been to blame. But the woman who saved Stuie hugged me. No words were spoken.

I later learned that Stuie was developing symptoms of Muscular Dystrophy. He had to fallen in the water, on his knees. I didn't know it then, but this was just the beginning of great decline for Stuie.

Essay 3:

Stuie had died. I graduated from high school. Daddy stopped speaking to me for most of the summer. Mom decided that my older brother and I needed relief from all the sadness. So she bought tickets for us to see Hulk Hogan at the Civic Center.

Daddy did drive us, chatting with Russell, and ignoring me. However, he silently handed me money for my brother and I to eat something, and buy what we wanted.

Russell loved all sports, including wrestling . And Hulk Hogan was his favorite wrestler. But my older brother educated me that most of it was for show. It seemed funny to me that a young man in a wheelchair wished to see this, but Russell enjoyed this show.

He had to use the bathroom during intermission so I had to take him into the ladies room. He was in a wheelchair and he needed me to hand him a urinal. I had to dump the contents out when he was done filling it.

But a lady came in on us and screamed she was calling the

cops . And she did. I started to cry. But Russell was calm. He explained to the police why he was there. The man was very compassionate. He lectured the woman sternly. She left us.

We went back to the show. Hulk Hogan noticed Russell, as we sat very close to the ring. He came down to greet us both. He chatted with Russell, who was beaming .

Russell asked me a favor, "Don't tell them what happened in the bathroom, just that we met the Hulk!"

Daddy talked to Russell, not to me. He was still deep in grief over Stuie's death. I was so close to Stuie that my presence reminded him of Stuie.

It was Mom who told Daddy it was unfair to ignore me like this. He was harming me. Daddy and I had been close as well until this tragedy. It would be two more months before Daddy spoke to me again.

But at least Russell had a happy memory that summer. I was grateful I had a small part in creating it.

Essay 4:

The Hebrew tutor yelled at my brother, Russell, out of frustration. Daddy rushed into the den where Russell sat in his chair. The house was too narrow for any wheelchair, and special chairs were more comfortable for the boys, both my brothers suffered from Duchenne Muscular Dystrophy.

"Why are you yelling at my son?"

"He isn't learning the material!"

"Screaming won't help him learn any better!"

The Hebrew teacher took offense that his methods were being challenged.

Mom came into the room next   "We don't pay you to make Russell sad. We pay you to help him learn!"

"He will never learn these lessons!"

Mom and Daddy both gestured for the man to leave.

But as he did, Russell said very solemnly, "I will learn the Hebrew with someone else!"

Mom found another tutor for Russell. Mr. Weiner was very learned, but a patient man. He did not yell at Russell, if he made a mistake, but encouraged him to try again.

So Russell did learn his Torah portion for his Bar Mitzvah. Russell, in fact, had a good singing voice. At his Bar Mitzvah, on the East Side of Providence, on Summit Avenue, near

Miriam Hospital, Russell was lifted onto the bima by Daddy, and sat next to the rabbi.

Russell sang his portion beautifully, with no noticeable mistakes. People who had not been invited came anyhow. Louie, the Kosher caterer, managed to have enough food for everyone.

It was a joyous day in October for my entire family. Because my parents believed in Russell. They did not see Muscular Dystrophy as what defined their sons. They saw it as an obstacle to overcome, not to be defeated by it.

And my parents helped both boys overcome many obstacles to be their best selves.

.

You have just read my version of events in the life of my family. But to really have a complete narrative, you need to read my Mom's version. It is what I think she would say.

Don''t consider which view is correct. They both tell the truth in different perspectives. They don't compete with each other, they compliment one another.

There is overlapping in some parts of course. It is actually interesting to relive the same time with a separate conclusion.

So here we go, with Mom's view of the story.

Walking with one foot
in front
of the other

"Walk With One Foot In Front Of The Other"
  By Cindy Halpern
Why I write in the first person for my late Mom matters greatly to me. I am obviously not her, I can not know every thought she had, and I will never able to relate everything that ever happened to her.
What I can do is show how she saw the world from her positive perspective. But more importantly, how her thinking influenced her doing something about creating change. She was a great believer in making new possibilities for not only herself, but others as well. And she proved that change can happen under the worst situations.
I am not Mom. I can never fill her big shoes. But I honor her memory by writing about her life. And somehow, I hope good comes from telling her story. That is what Mom would want.
In Memory of Tina Korner Chernick
((1921-2013).
May her memory be a blessing.

Chapter 1: My Beginning

I was born in Vienna, in a hospital, in 1921.
My parents were glad of my birth, but a bit surprised.
My siblings were all much older than me, and all was
not well with two of them.
But I became their youngest child, and the only one
born in Vienna. The former ways of Bukovina, where
my family came from before my birth, were not to be a
part of my present.
The fact that I was born in a hospital, not at home,
reflected that. A doctor delivered me, not a midwife. So
the modern medical community was my beginning.
Of course, Mom was a hausfrau. Her work was rearing

children as well as cooking and cleaning. My father's parents lived with us when I was very young. My grandmother especially spoke Yiddish.

But Papa wanted German to be my first language. He reasoned that my life in Vienna depended upon me speaking German well, as a native, which is what I was. My talent for speaking German correctly and talking Yiddish nearly as well let my father know that I was good in languages.

But it was more than that which led to me going to private school. I was incredibly bright in every area. My siblings, being much older, and working, let Papa see me as different from them.

Well, my brother, Lazar, did not work. My parents said Polio made it so he could not walk. So he stayed home. But he had many books he studied from. I often sat with him, and he drilled me on French, mathematics, German Literature.

Papa saw how fast I learned everything . And Lazar was proud of his little sister, me! It was he who told Papa I had a different destiny to fulfill. Papa always respected Lazar, despite him not walking.

But there was also Klara, the oldest. She was 14 when I was born, but she acted wildly, I am told. I really don't remember her well at all. When I was 4, she was sent away to live elsewhere.   There were whispers about her, nothing I was suppose to know. I begged Lazar to tell me about Klara. He hesitated of course. Papa trusted Lazar. But I pleaded to learn about her. So in a very low tone, he told me. Klara was never right from the start. I wasn't the only one born in a hospital. Klara had been born in a hospital in Sadogora, back in Bukovina, in 1907. She was the first born, but the pregnancy went wrong. Mama was too thin, couldn't gain any weight.

And before labor began, Mama got very sick. Her rich father insisted she go to the hospital for the birth. And immediately, the doctors said the baby would never be right.

Klara lagged behind all her milestones. But worse than that, she became angry easily. She would try to hurt her younger siblings. Regina was just 13 months younger, Abraham was 2 years younger, Mina was 4 years younger, and Lazar was 5 years younger.

But the other children protected each other, not letting Klara do great harm.

With my birth, Klara was enraged. Someone always had to watch Klara carefully. One day, Klara got to me, lifted me up, and tried to harm me. Regina, who now assumed the role of eldest daughter, stopped her. Papa decided Klara belonged in a special place where she could be cared for. At 16, Klara was placed at the Steinhof, in the 13th district.

No mention of her was made, there were no pictures of her. But Lazar said Papa and Abe visited her sometimes.

But now I was nearly 6. I was obviously very bright. So Papa arranged for me to take an entrance examination for a scholarship to private school. It was the only way I could go. I had a perfect score so I was admitted.

I told Papa I wanted to become a medical doctor from when I was very young. Because maybe I could find a cure for Lazar.

Papa seemed uneasy when I first said this. I didn't know why. Then he asked me if I would be willing to always study. I could only have a career, never marry.

I understood. I still wanted to do it anyhow.

Papa explained that if at anytime I couldn't get great grades or score perfectly on examinations, I could not be a doctor. So I worked even harder to do well. And I always did well. Never did I not have perfect scores In all my studies.

Because I was a Jew and a girl, I had to be the best.

Chapter 2: Lazar

Lazar worked with me to perfect my studies. He continued to drill me. I easily caught on. Papa was pleased with both of us. Lazar was very smart. Had he not got sick, he could have been the doctor. Maybe Papa would not want me to be one then.

Papa was a Hebrew teacher who prepared many boys for their Bar Mitzvah. He could speak many languages, too, besides Hebrew. His German was perfectly spoken, so was Yiddish. But he knew Rumanian as well as Polish, some Russian, I think as well. Also French and Latin.

I needed to learn Greek to go to medical school. I had to study that mostly on my own. Papa and Lazar did not know that language at all.

Science and Math came easily to me. I could do Algebra in my early grades. And learning biology was so fun!

But Lazar seemed worse to me. He coughed too much. His posture was bad. Papa and Mama got very upset when Lazar seemed to struggle to breathe. So they sent him to Lainz Neuromuscular Hospital.

I never saw him again!

I asked many questions how polio could suddenly worsened like this? Papa was furious at me. He never got mad at me, but he did this time.

Mama cried so hard, it scared me. My sister, Regina, took me to Prater Park for the afternoon. Regina was always kind to me, never yelled. She was like a second mother to me, especially when Lazar got sick, which was often.

Mama tended to Lazar in every way. She even lifted him. She sat with him every minute when he was ill.

But when my sister and I returned home, all the mirrors were covered.

My brother, Abe, was the one who told us in hushed tones that Lazar had died in the hospital. But I screamed so loudly. Polio did not progress like this once you survived it!

Papa charged at me like a wild animal! But Regina and Abe rushed me away, out of the house. They took me to our Aunt and Uncle's home by trolley. My Aunt was also named Regina and my Uncle was William. They had 4 children, my cousins.

They were very kind. I stayed with them when Regina and Abe had to return home. I would not be allowed to go to Lazar's funeral at all. And I was not wanted at the Shiva.

I was not to go to school that week at all. But my Aunt and Uncle treated me so kindly. Uncle William taught me a few words in Polish. Aunt Regina baked me Sacher Torte and I played with my cousins.

They lived in a beautiful home. They even had a Vienna Regulator, a special clock only wealthy people could afford to buy. I admired it so. They had a piano their children played. I listened to them playing classical musical.

Papa had taken me to the opera. I got dressed up for it. It was usually for my birthday or Hanukkah. It was a special treat for me.

Now I returned home. Papa was no longer angry at me, just very sad. All of Lazar's belongings were gone, except for one item. I went into his former room and saw something had fallen behind the bed. It was a picture of him with his friends.

Chapter 3: Mina

I rushed into my room I shared with my much older sisters. My sister, Mina, saw what I held. Mina was beautifully dressed in the latest fashions. She was a seamstress by profession. Her blonde hair was cut in the latest trend.

She gently looked at the picture.

"I will help you hide it".

Mina and Papa always fought about everything. Mina was very modern. She did not accept tradition well.

So knowing Papa would not want me to have this picture, Mina wanted me to have it.

Mina sat down on her bed and told me to sit next to her.

"I was not allowed to be here for anything! I loved Lazar so much!"

Mina held my hand, "I didn't agree with that. If I had a say, you would have stayed!"

"Can you tell me what it was like?"

"I was not allowed at his funeral either, but did not go to work. I was here for the Shiva. It was awful. Mama never stopped crying. But then at the end of 7 days, Papa told Mom the grieving period was over. She had to stop crying. Papa took all of Lazar's things away. Mama wasn't allowed to keep anything.

He did the same thing when Klara died."

"She died? No one told me!"

"Last year in February. "

"As if she never existed at all!"

Chapter 4: Moving Forward

Lazar was dead, but we had to act like nothing had happened. Klara died, and we pretended like she never lived at all.

But I still had my studies. Papa did not take that away.

Right after Lazar's death, my grandparents were placed at the Jewish Home of the Aged, and we moved. It was a nicer apartment. But no one there knew about Lazar or Klara. We weren't allowed to speak of them to anyone.

I broke the rule once when Regina took me to visit my grandparents. Grandfather couldn't remember anything much at all. But Bubbe did. She let me speak about my brother and sister.

She especially told me that Klara had very dark hair, but light eyes. She could play piano as a young child in Bukovina. But she became upset easily. She never went to school at all.

But Lazar was the brightest student at school. Everyone liked him so much. Even as he walked funny, his friends remained loyal.

I was confused and asked about polio.

Regina smiled, then said we had to go now.Bubbe nodded, said that was perhaps best.

So I went to Mina to ask her more about how Lazar got polio. Mina seemed frightened.

"Even I must respect Papa about this."

So I had to let it go.

I went on with my studies. And Papa did take me again to see opera for Hanukkah.

Mom was never quite the same after my brother and sister died. But she would say nothing about them. There was no talk about my sisters marrying. They worked their jobs. Mina always had boyfriends, but oddly no marriage proposals. Regina never dated at all.

Chapter 5: Abe

But Abe had someone named Magda. He fought with Papa about her. Magda's father was a Jew, but her mother was not. That made her unacceptable in Papa's eyes.

Abe didn't care. He was going to marry her anyhow.

But then Abe collapsed from pain one day. He was rushed to the hospital. He had to have his appendix removed, or he would die.

Uncle William, who was rich, paid for a surgeon to save Abe. My parents could not have got the best doctor. The surgeon saved Abe.

After that, Papa always spoke kindly of his brother-in-law.

But Abe's recovery was slow.

Papa received news he feared would harm his son so he said nothing at first. When Abe got better, Papa told him, Magda was dead. She got hit by a trolley car.

Abe was depressed for a long time. He vowed never to marry now. Papa didn't argue with him at all. It seemed odd that he didn't care there would be no grandchildren. For I, as a doctor, would never marry. And Regina, Abe, and Mina would never marry either. Mina always said obeying a husband was not for her anyhow. She prefer dating, riding motorcycles, skiing, which boyfriends paid for, and wearing beautiful dresses.

Chapter 6: Briefly Regina, then Sickness

Regina probably never talked to any man in a romantic way. She had friends from work she went on outings, with Papa's permission of course. They weren't Jewish, but Regina promised she never dated anyone.

Regina always told the truth. These people were just friends.

Then I got very sick with Scarlet Fever. I was taken away to the hospital. Mama and Papa weren't allowed to see me. I was forced to go to a Catholic Hospital with crosses everywhere.

The nuns tried to teach me about their beliefs in case I died. Ordinarily, I was a very polite child, but not to these nuns. I yelled in Latin to them to leave me alone. Then I screamed in Greek, then Yiddish, French, and German.

They were shocked at how bright I was. They actually stopped preaching to me.
I got well and went home.

Abe, Mina, Regina, Mama, and Papa all greeted with me cake and presents. Everyone stayed home all day to celebrate my homecoming.

All my clothes remained where they belonged. Nothing was put into boxes. They all believed I would survive.

Chapter 7: Back To Normal

I worked even harder at my studies. All my scores remained perfect, as always. My teachers said I was the brightest student in the whole 9th district.

While I was in the hospital, my grandfather had died. But it was no secret, no hushed tones. All his special documents came to Papa, his son. Papa openly spoke of him, the great teacher of Sadogora in the Hasidic tradition. We weren't Hasidic Jews in Vienna.

Papa was mainstream Orthodox. Wealthy Jews hired him to tutor their sons. Papa dressed in suits always. He wore a yamulka under his hat. His mustache was well trimmed, there was no beard.
Papa had blonde hair and blue eyes. He might have passed as a non-Jew, had he wished to.

I wondered how we came away from being traditional to being more mainstreamed? Of course, we kept Kosher in the house, all Jewish holidays observed. But my hair was braided like Viennese girls, my dresses just average length. Mina wore modern dresses. Maybe Regina wore more frumpy clothes, by choice.

Mama didn't push for the old ways practiced before they came to Vienna in 1917, during the Great War. Papa served in the Austrian Army with pride. He even became an officer who soldiers respected.

My grandparents had dressed old fashioned, but no one else did. And even then, my grandparents hadn't complained about changes.

Abe told me how the Austrian soldiers protected my family as they boarded a train to Vienna. The Russians were invading, and Jews knew life would be bad under Russian Rule. They were grateful to be going to Vienna, to remain Austrian subjects.

My whole family was glad I was born in Vienna. I could not be forced to leave Austria as having been born there.

So Papa made sure I was raised Viennese, although also to be a good Jew. I could better the world as a doctor. Papa seemed relieved I would not marry. It seemed odd, but I never questioned it. It is why he let me study.

It was Mama who seemed sad there would be no grandchildren. She had hoped Abe at least would. She wanted Magda to convert to Judaism. It was the one time she and Papa disagreed.

I heard her utter that no harm could come if Abe had children. It made no sense to me at all.

I went to my best friend's house sometimes. Edith's father was very rich, even more wealthy than Uncle William. They had servants. Their house was a mansion. Edith went to my school because she was rich. She was not the excellent student I was. Edith's Mom liked to speak French to me. Her father talked mathematics with me. They were very fond of me. They told Papa they could pay for my books at the University of Vienna. My scholarship would not pay for that.

It was time to take the biggest test of all. A full year before entrance, I had to take this examination to be accepted to the University of Vienna on full scholarship. I had to score at least 98% correct in every section, in Greek, Latin, Anatomy, Chemistry, and Physics. And even French and German because I was on scholarship.

I was very confident. Uncle William bought me a suit to wear for testing. Edith's father bought me a brief case. Mina gave me a blouse, Regina made me a hat.

I looked the part of a future university student. I was even allowed to wear stockings and heels!

My scores came back quickly. I scored a 100% on every section. I just needed to complete one more year of classical high school. I had straight A's in every subject.

Chapter 8: The Nazis in Vienna

But what happened next changed my entire life. I couldn't believe it. I was kicked out of school. It didn't matter that I had perfect grades, had never been rude, or disobedient. I was a Jew and no matter how smart I was, I was considered inferior, not worthy of an education.

All my hard work, from first grade until a year before I was to attend university, was to end like this? I got very angry. But Mama, who never got involved with my studies, told me, "Tina, you walk one foot in front of the other. You can never go back, only forward".

Papa was the philosophical one, not Mama. Yet, she gave me a saying that I could use to guide my life. These were difficult days, and I needed to somehow stay positive.

So even as I had to face the loss of the life I had known, I had to look towards the future.

My brother, Abe, was coming home, and had just reached the courtyard, when Nazi thugs seized him. They took him away first to prison, then to a place called Dachau. It was in Germany, near Munich.

Papa went to see his army friends. He could have been arrested, as Jews were restricted to where they could go. But he still had his trolley pass. He did not look Jewish. And our name Korner is German sounding. Mama was frightened Papa would never come back. My sisters, Mina, Regina, and I huddled around her, praying Papa would return unharmed.

He did come home somehow. He didn't know what could be done, but his friends in war were now professional Nazis. They didn't necessarily believe the lies told about Jews. They wanted to have good jobs and did what they needed to do. That didn't make them right, but they felt Papa was an honorable man. They served with him in war and liked him a lot.

Meanwhile, we were thrown out of our apartment and made to move to another one, by the police station, on the 4th floor. We rarely left it. Papa went to get food during the few hours allotted to get rations.

Mama had no curtains to cover windows. So we saw Jewish men beaten at the police station. At least I did. The others looked away. I wanted to remember it all.

I never doubted that somehow we would survive. I had great knowledge in many areas. Instead of using my intelligence to study, I needed to use it to help us survive.

Papa's friends became useful to us in several ways.

When The Night of the Broken Glass came in November, Papa was forced onto the pavement. But he rushed away to the synagogue that was on fire. He tried to save the Torahs. He was arrested, his mug shot taken. But then, he was just let go.

He came home, shaken, although he tried not to show it. He was sure his army buddies somehow got him released from custody.

Things got even worse. We were frightened we would all be taken away in the night. Uncle William had been a Polish citizen when he came to Vienna after the Great War. He was forced to return there. My father's sister, Aunt Regina, and their children went with him.

Papa could do nothing to help them at all.

But, then came word that Abe, who had been transferred to a worse place called Buchenwald, was being released.

Even then, it was uncertain what would happen. He rushed home to Vienna, just for a few hours. Papa gave him all our pictures to take with him. Then he was gone. It was hoped he would somehow make it to the land of our people. But it was likely he could be recaptured, even killed.

My grandmother in the Jewish nursing home had died. We were told she fell down some stairs. But Bubbe couldn't walk anymore. How could she fall down stairs?

Papa believed the Nazis pushed her to her death.

He and the rabbi risked a Jewish burial for her. None of us could go. But I hadn't been allowed to go to any funerals anyhow, not for my brother or sister, grandfather, and now not for Bubbe either.

We were in great danger. Papa could not pretend otherwise. If we didn't leave Vienna soon, we would all die.

But, Papa's friends told him the Italian border was secretly open for three days only in August. We had to dash to the train station somehow. Everything worth anything had to be sold, nothing could be saved.

Chapter 9: Italy

So off we went on the train to Milano. I watched as we passed through the Austrian countryside. There was no words spoken among us. We were fearful during the whole ride. Afraid we would be thrown off at the next station, we just prayed we would make it into Italy.

We crossed the border without incident. Papa's friends had been right. The Italians were letting Jews like us into their country.

But all was not well. Milano officials said we could not remain. Too many Jews were already here. Yet, we weren't sent back to Austria. We were told we were allowed to go to Genoa the next day. We were processed, our pictures were taken. But it was for ID, not a mug shot.

Mama was very afraid. We all were, but Mina,

Papa and I stayed calm. Regina was also frightened. She always had a schedule to live by. She took me to school by trolley, she worked, then picked me up. Sometimes, she went with friends into Wienerwald, Vienna Woods. She helped Mama get ready for Shabbat. And that was her life.

Now we faced great uncertainty. Regina tried hard to be brave. I was turning 18 within a couple of weeks. But Regina was 13 years older than me. She was to be 31 in November. It was easier for me than for her to adjust.

We went to Genoa, and there was no trouble at all. In fact, we felt nearly normal again. We rented an apartment at Via Colombo. Papa got a job immediately to help Rabbi Ricardo at the small synagogue. Papa would again teach Hebrew. Mina got a job as seamstress. Regina sold hats at a shop.

Believe it or not, I was permitted to do my senior year studies at high school. No, it wasn't like school in Vienna. It wasn't as advantaged at all. But, it was important. I was learning to speak Italian quite quickly. My knowledge of Latin really helped! And I made Italian friends easily. Tina sounded like an Italian name to them. I had dark hair like them. And I was very friendly, too.

I was allowed to walk anywhere I wished. It felt so good after being confined for more than a year in Vienna in that horrible apartment near the police station. So I walked every day down to the port to see ships come and go. Sometimes, my classmates invited me to have gelato with them. Mama told me to go with them. Papa was busy working at synagogue, and Mama decided what I was allowed to do.

Mina began to have Italian boyfriends. Papa would not have approved. But again, Mama allowed it. Mama just wanted a peaceful life again. She wanted no arguments among us.

Regina just worked and came home. She made no friends her at all, although she learned a little Italian and was friendly with customers who bought hats.

Life was good like this for about a year. But then came the bombs from the British. We were allowed into the air raid shelters with our neighbors. Regina and Mama screamed as bombs dropped around us. Again, Papa, Mina, and I were brave. We just hoped we would survive.

Then bad news found us. No longer were we allowed to stay in Genoa! But worst of all, Papa was being sent to an internment camp in the North. At least, he remained in Italy. The rest of us were being sent far South, to a mountainous village, called Oppido Lucano.

Mama and Regina both cried bitterly. What if we never saw Papa again? But I believed we would. Unlike the Austrians, the Italians remained polite towards us, telling us we would be fed and cared for.

My Italian language skills became very strong. I was quite fluent in fact. I knew I could be a big help to us all, except Papa.

So we said good-bye. We went to our separate trains. I held Mama's hand, telling her what she had told me, to walk one foot in front of the other. I would need to remain strong and confident for all our sake.

We made it to the small village. The policeman was told by me that since I spoke Italian, I was the one who would be reporting to the police station daily.

There was no need for the others to come. These Italian police were reasonable. They did not threaten us with harm. They were cordial. They simply needed to keep track of us.

But we were free to walk the town. So I walked the town every single day. I spoke to everyone I saw, whether it were men, women, and children. When they heard me speak their language well, they did not treat me like a stranger anymore.

Many welcomed me into their homes. I would not eat pork. Papa wasn't with us in this village, I could have done as I wished. But Papa's values were mostly what I believed.

Mina also attracted attention. Still beautiful, men liked her. But her Italian skills were not nearly as good as mine. So she had to be careful. She was a bit wild, but never out of control. She let men kiss her, hug her, but nothing more than that.

Then I met Benjamin. He was young and handsome. He liked me a lot. He wasn't Jewish. I would never marry him, but he became my boyfriend. I did nothing dishonorable, but certainly, Papa would not approve.

Even Regina did not lecture me. We depended upon the goodwill of these people in this town to survive.

And there were some hard times for us to face. The police told us German Nazis were coming soon. We needed to find places to hide. They could not help us, but they would not tell the Nazis we were here.

So the priest brought us to the church's wine cellar. He gave us blankets and food. We were to be quiet. He showed us where to relieve ourselves. We couldn't be embarrassed. Otherwise, we would die. I saw what was done at the Viennese police station. People were beaten to death.

I knew, should we be captured, we would be treated like those other Jews were in Vienna. So we had to avoid being discovered.

I worried about poor Papa. But he was allowed to write letters to us. He wasn't being beaten and he was fed. The conditions weren't great, but they were livable for now.

And then, we were hidden again, at the cemetery. There were above ground vaults we had to go into. We had to disregard the coffin there. It was awful, worse than the wine cellar, but there was no choice. But when there were no German Nazis about, these people in the town fed us. We had to sleep in hallways, not bedrooms. But many warm blankets were placed down. We even had pillows to rest our heads about.

Food supplies became less for everyone. But whatever food there was, it was shared with us. There was little medicine now, we had to guard our health. Mama got arthritis, but nothing could be done about it. It could get very damp high in the mountains. I applied warmth to her knees when possible.

Then we received a letter from Papa. Finally, some good news. He was to join us here in the village very soon. He was born in 1880. He was now 64. He was considered elderly, no longer any threat.

So he came to be with us. He got old looking, rather fragile in fact. But his appearance helped secure his release from the internment camp.

Our relief was very short lived. The police told us the German Nazis knew of our presence in the village. They were coming to get us!

But these good Italian offered us a solution, not a great one, but better than the fate that awaited us in German hands. We were to surrender to Italian Fascists. They would not kill us. The Allies were now close in North Africa and Sicily, since we were deep in the South of Italy. If we could just survive long enough for the Allied arrival, we would live.

So we were given protection by Italian Fascists on yet another train ride. This time we went to Ferramonti Concentration Camp. It really was more like an internment camp. It was fenced, separated from any town. Food was very limited for everyone, there was no medication available.

But surprisingly, it was me who got Malaria. I got very sick. A fellow prisoner, I never knew his name, gave me his food rations. He was Italian and Catholic. Even in my weakened state, I asked him why he was here.
He told me he was a homosexual. He had been caught. He was jailed here and there, until he came here.
I never met a homosexual before. Such talk was never spoken in my home in Vienna. I had no concept of that, except in the Bible. It was mentioned about Lot's family living among evil. But this man gave me his food. He was not evil at all, but very good in fact. Even Papa recognized this good deed.

The man died and was buried in the camp's field. I was sure I would be buried next. With my medical knowledge, I knew I was dying.

Then the Allies arrived. The British came first, then the American followed. They were made aware of the dying Jewish young woman, me. They immediately put me into an ambulance and rushed me to their field medical compound. They had the medicine I required to live.

Chapter 10: America

It took a few weeks, but I got better. My family joined me with some news to share. We were to temporarily be moved to America. A warship would take us there. But we were to be there only until war's end. We were to return to Vienna.

We were all horrified. How could we ever go back to Vienna? To live among killers. But Papa advised us not to think so far ahead. We had to get through the rest of the war first.

We had no idea whether Abe ever made it to the Holy Land. We hoped he had, but we had no way to know. We prayed he was at least alive somewhere.

So we went on a ship called the Henry Gibbons. There were many American soldiers, but we were separated from them. We had quarters we shared with other Jews. Some had been with us in Ferramonti. Others had hidden in Italy. They were from Yugoslavia.

We kept mostly to ourselves, or at least with Viennese Jews. The Yugoslavia Jews disliked us greatly.

There was a woman named Ruth Gruber. She came to be with us. She worked for the Secretary of the Interior in the United States. She wanted to teach us to speak English. I learned very quickly. She saw I was very bright. She used me to help her teach others.

We arrived on American shores. But we were treated roughly. We were sprayed down like animals, given ID tags to wear around our necks. We were placed on a train.

When we arrived at Fort Ontario, we were in shock to see the barbed wire fence. Some people began to cry, including Mama and Regina. Papa and I were very angry.

Ruth was with us. She tried to calm us down. We were to be fed, not harmed. There would be medical care. But I told Ruth in German this was not right, for all we had suffered, to be treated like this.

She agreed with me. She said she would fight for our rights. I believed she would try. Whether she would succeed was questionable.

So inside the camp we went. My family shared

quarters with a few other families. American soldiers spoke to me, as I already could speak some English, although I was not yet fluent.

We were Viennese, we were used to the cold. I had lived in the mountains of Italy for 4 years as well. But some of the older ones were always cold. I felt so sorry for them. And it was all for nothing anyhow. We were to be shipped back to Europe.

But we made the best of it.
Ruth came with exciting news for some of us. I wasn't sure if I was included or not. Schools would be open to us from elementary to college. It was now December of 1944. I was already 23 years old. I did finish high school in Italy, just barely.

Ruth said I lost time in school through no fault of my own. I had done so well in learning Italian, now English. I could go to college at Oswego! I was so happy. I loved learning, I always loved school from when I was very young.

There were restrictions. We were taken to school daily and we returned when classes ended. We were not free to roam the town. The Italians allowed me to roam their town, but the Americans did not!

I was angry. It was Mama who told me again, walk one foot in front of the other. So I was to make the most of going to an American college.

And I did. I was allowed to choose my course of study. I would study Chemistry and Physics of course. There would be no medical school for me now, but at least I could study science!

It was so easy for me. I did not let on that this American college repeated what I already learned in Vienna, in classical high school. I got perfect grades, even better than the young men in my class.

   They liked the pretty blonde girl better than me. She was not nearly as smart as me. I had to let it go, my jealousy. I was never suppose to marry. But with my medical career now never launched, I wonder whether I had to rethink that.

Eleanor Roosevelt came to visit us in camp. My English was quite good now so I spoke to her. She praised me, said I spoke English eloquently. I told her I was studying Chemistry and Physics. She wasn't shocked at all. Ruth had told her about me. Mrs. Roosevelt told me she was fighting so we could stay. So was Ruth.

   I began to believe it was possible we might stay. Papa wasn't so sure. Regina was frightened. Mama had calmed down a bit. Mina hoped we would remain in America.

The war was ending when we got word Roosevelt had died. Many were upset, feared what Harry Truman might do with us. I worried whether Mrs. Roosevelt would still try to help us now that her husband was dead.

   She came again to see us in the camp. She said she was talking to President Truman about our situation. Ruth came as well. Her boss, the Secretary of the Interior, was on our side. The problem was there was a strict small quota for immigration. We were stateless, here in this camp. We weren't counted as immigrants, only temporary refugees.

   But Harry Truman saw films of displaced persons camps in Europe. He would not send us to those places. He found a solution to solve the problem.

Ruth explained that a bus would take some of us over Lake Ontario into Canada from Niagara Falls. We were to be processed, listed as immigrants coming into the US from Canada. Our time in Oswego counted towards nothing. We were considered nearly arrived, on February 3, 1946.

Most of us qualified to stay, a few did not. A couple were sent back to Europe, but we were safe. A family unit was considered more stable. I spoke English, was educated and employable. My two sisters could also work. Papa would try to teach Hebrew again, but it was doubtful. He was now to be 65, and he looked it.

Chapter 11: Rhode Island

Mama had distant relatives in Providence, Rhode Island. The Kleins were likely third cousins .

We took a train from Buffalo to Providence. But our reception was not what we hoped for. Adelaide Klein, the daughter, was closer to my age. She spoke kindly to me, but her parents were quite abrupt.

I had to translate what they said. We were to get a tenement immediately. We had to find jobs at once. They would give us the security deposit, but nothing more could be expected.

So we went to Dudley Street, to a third floor apartment. Mama could hardly climb stairs. She would have to stay upstairs mostly. Papa immediately searched for a teaching position. No one wanted to hire him.

Regina, Mina, and I went to the Cathedral Jewelry Factory and got work immediately.

But many there spoke little or no English. I was used to translate a lot. I helped people fill forms out, I explained about wages. My sisters both were stuck doing piece work.

The owner liked me from the start. He knew of a better position for me at the Jewish funeral home. I refused it. I did not want to be among the dead. So he told me about a laboratory position at Rhode Island Hospital. He said I could try it, come back if I didn't like it.

I easily could do lab work with my knowledge of Chemistry. I did well. But the German workers, not Jewish, made fun of me. I got so angry. Never before did I have such rage. I called them filthy names in German. They screamed and cried. I did not care. I repeated what I said. I didn't, wouldn't, couldn't work with them.

I went back to the factory. My boss had me continue translation. But I would find another way out of this life, into better circumstances.

I went to Rhodes on the Pawtucket, a place to meet men that was respectable. My sister, Mina, accompanied me. She was still beautiful in her late 30's. But her prospects were few. She felt I had great possibilities still in my middle 20's.

And men did date me. They found be charming, pretty, and intelligent. But they dated me but a few times. They were fearful I had older parents who relied on me heavily. They did not want burdens like them to support. Then I met Elliott. He was Jewish of course. He appreciated me for my looks and intelligence. He liked me.

He met my parents. He thought he could get serious with me. But he spoke of a longer engagement. I didn't like that at all.

I was now approaching 28. In those days, that was no longer considered youthful. Papa got nervous whenever I spoke of marrying and having children. I actually argued with him. I would not have a career now as a doctor. Those were old dreams that could not be fulfilled. I only had completed one year of college. There was no money for more. I was now well beyond the age of returning to college.

Did he expect me to toil away in a factory?

Papa said I could find better work. I was smart, knew English, I had excellent skills in math and science. I would work my way up to a new career.

But it wasn't what I wanted anymore. I wanted a real home, security, a better life. A good marriage was what I needed, and deserved.

Papa just stayed angry at the topic. Mama had become confused by now, couldn't see well either. Regina wanted me to listen to Papa. Mina said I could do as I wished.

I kept on dating. Mrs. Lowry was my friend at the factory. She was also an Austrian Jew. She knew of a man in East Providence who wanted to meet someone.

She warned me he was 10 years older than me. He had lost most of his hair. But he had a profession. It was a bit different, but he made money legally.

So David Chernick came to call. He had a car he drove me in. I liked riding in it. He took me to Roger Williams Park. He spoke a little German. He served in the American Army in Bavaria.

But my English was much better than his German.

He liked me well enough. He wasn't handsome at all. But he was kind. He bought me popcorn and ice cream without any fuss.

He said he wanted a wife. He was nearly 38 now. He made a decent living. He expected he would make a good living soon. He could give me whatever I needed. I could quit working for good. He would always provide for me. I never would have to beg for anything. If I wanted new clothes, I could have them. He would try to teach me to drive and buy me a car.

I said yes to him. We would marry very soon, in a synagogue.

I didn't like his mother much. His father thought I was beautiful. His sisters were mostly okay with me.

Papa was furious. Mina and Regina had to calm him down. Mama just hugged me. She was too confused to argue with Papa now.

Papa said he and Mama and my sisters would come to the marriage ceremony at synagogue, but not the dinner at my new in-laws home.

I accepted that.

David and I were married at Temple Beth Shalom. I only wore a suit. There was no time for anything else. David gave me the money for my suit, blouse, shoes, and hat. I could tell he was really going to be generous to me.

The dinner was horrible. Our wedding cake was a birthday cake for a niece. But David would let no one insult me. His mother tried, but failed. David totally took my side so she stopped. My father -in-law saying I was so beautiful probably didn't help matters.

We took a weekend in New York City. We stayed at a beautiful hotel. David took me shopping for more clothes. As a joke, David had me sit on Santa's lap, as this was late November.

When we returned, David bought a tenement. We lived on the first floor, our renter lived on the second floor. David did try to teach me to drive. I got my license, but I proved I could not drive without screaming out of fear.

Then I found out, I was pregnant. David was delighted of course. So was I. My mother-in-law gave me the cold shoulder. But Papa's reaction was worst of all.

Papa screamed at me. He said I had made a terrible mistake. David took me home. He would not have me get upset.

The pregnancy was not going well. I could not gain weight. David made sure I ate. His sisters came over with nice meals. Regina and Mina brought food as well. Even my father-in-law gave me food.

My doctor was very worried about the development of the baby. David said he loved me, even if we lost this child. Papa became very nervous now. He even cried. Papa came to me. He was very sad. He said he let it all go too far. He prayed it would be a girl. But even then, he was fearful.

I began to wonder what he was talking about. He was not telling me something. I had no idea what it could be he was hiding.

Mina began to act oddly. I was afraid Regina would be the one to go mad. She was overly sensitive and sheltered. But Regina remained as she always was, dependable, reliable, working, cooking, or cleaning.

Mina began to talk about the past constantly, about what happened to us in Vienna. She spoke of Lazar, too, what a beautiful boy he was, so smart, so kindly. I asked her when he came down with polio. She screamed so loudly that he never had polio.

I was frightened. Of course he had polio, he stopped walking, he even died at 18.

I went to see my doctor. I gained a little weight at least. He didn't seem hopeful. I thought if this child did not live, there would be others. David promised he would still love me.

I went into labor. The delivery itself went normally. My vital signs were stable, I was safe from harm. But I saw my little girl. She was small, but not terribly so. But she didn't respond like most babies do. She wasn't in any physical danger. Yet, something seemed wrong.

Papa came to see her. He didn't say much at first, not to upset me. He waited sometime in fact to say what he thought.

Then he said that Regina would come help me with my baby after work. I accepted the offer. I was new at this. Regina helped with all of us when we were younger.

Papa, meanwhile, asked David if we could find out what Abe's fate was. My husband asked his father what could be done. He contacted Senator Pell, who had big connections.

Abe was found living in Haifa, Israel, as a plumber. Contact was made with him. We were full of joy that Abe had also survived.

But Papa wrote many letters, saying I now had a little girl. He was desperate for Abe to come to America.

Chapter 12: Abe Comes To America

In 1951, my brother arrived. Mina and Regina went with David to New York Harbor. Mina was still acting crazy. Her beauty was gone. Regina had aged, too. She was 43, she looked older. But Regina remained sane. Mina was not.

Abe came to my home. He was 42 by now. But he still looked handsome and strong. Gone was the teenager he knew me to be. But he said I was a beauty at 30.

But he looked at Anita, my child, and looked away.

Anita did respond differently to everything, but she was not deformed or sickly.

Regina was there and explained she helped me with Anita. Abe needed to work to support our parents.

Abe had been sponsored by Hasbro Toy Company in Pawtucket. He had a job as a machinist immediately.

He moved our parents and two sisters to a better apartment on Prairie Avenue. He had his own room. Our sisters shared another room, then our parents had their own room. The apartment was near everything. Bus routes were there, as was a synagogue and Kosher shops.

Papa praised Abe for coming and helping us. I was glad, too. Abe took me out sometimes, just the two of us. My husband was always pleased and welcomed Abe being a good brother to me. I could tell Abe my struggles with Anita.

She wouldn't sleep well. David took her for rides to calm her. She liked her Daddy, but not so much me. She was fussy, she cried a lot. She didn't learn easily. Her physical development was okay. Abe had a far away look. Then he added Regina was available to help. Abe would work overtime so Regina could work slightly less and be with me and the baby more.

I should have asked questions, I didn't. Maybe I didn't want to know the truth.

David got us a summer place down by the water. Anita and I spent time there. Anita was slightly calmer. But, I was glad when David joined us. Anita responded to him much better.

Then I found out I was pregnant again. Papa became very nervous. Even Regina didn't seem happy.

Mina became more crazy. She underwent shock treatment that knocked her teeth out, but failed to help her.

Mina met a man named Albert. He saw her wander the streets in a long dress, a hat, and shopping bag in summertime.

Albert was German -American. He fought as an American soldier in World War 1, on the opposite side of Papa.
But Papa liked Albert and trusted him. Albert proposed Mina living with him as a roommate. Nothing romantic at all. Mina would pay no rent. She could come and go as she pleased.

Regina really needed a break from Mina. Regina worked her job, helped with Anita, and our parents. Listening to Mina's crazy talk was too hard for her.

Papa agreed to the arrangement. Mama was very confused by now. She spoke of Klara when she hadn't before. Papa just ignored such talk.

Then Hurricane Carol roared through Rhode Island. David had been Downtown. He was a bail bondman. He had been at the courthouse. There was no word of him at all. Anita roamed outside. I went to get her back in the house. But a dog grabbed at my child. I picked her up, but she struggled against me. I took a terrible fall.

Our tenant saw that and came running, to help my child and me.
There was blood all over me!

He called the rescue squad to come, got Regina over to take Anita.

My father-in-law rushed to the hospital. There was no word about David so he felt it was his duty to come. Papa didn't come at all. But I was very sick. The doctors had to operate on me.

Even my mother-in-law came to the hospital. Everyone was frightened I would die!

I pulled through, but the pregnancy had ended terribly.

David was found safe, in a high building. The police brought him to my side.

He cried. He told me I could have no more children. I had been badly injured. I was fearful of my marriage. I knew Anita was not normal. There was no denying it now after what happened.
But David said he loved me so much. We would make do with Anita. If Regina couldn't help, he would hire help.

I cried bitterly, Anita was to become like Klara, locked away, forgotten. David promised me we would not do that to our child!

Papa came to see me once I came home. I confronted him about Klara! He trembled. Yes, it was true, Anita was like Klara had been. Only Regina and Papa could handle her. Mama never could. That is why Regina could help me now.

I asked him why at 16 Klara was sent away. Papa cried because Klara tried to kill me, toss me out of the window. I was 4 years old. Mina, Regina, and Abe had all stopped her.

Papa took her to the Steinhof. Abe and he visited her sometimes, when she was calm. She had been only mildly retarded, but very emotional. She was a danger to me, maybe in time she would kill me.

And 5 years later, her death was listed as pneumonia. But Papa was suspicious. There was something sinister that had happened.

In Vienna, if word got out, we were all be

stained by Klara. So everything was kept quiet. I wanted to go to medical school, my sisters and brother had jobs. We needed to function.

But David had money, Regina would help. My child would not be sent away.

I decided to volunteer at the March of Dimes, to join the synagogue sisterhood. David would hire help to relieve me when Regina wasn't available.

Anita had to go to public school now. She couldn't keep up, but we begged for the school to let her stay.

Anita made friends with a Chinese girl named Nancy Chin. Nancy was a nice child who always kept Anita calm. Her big Chinese family let Anita come over to play alot.

Meanwhile, Albert kept Mina with him. Mina had been of average intelligence, very sociable, and beautiful in Vienna. Only the last few years did she become crazy.

I decided the doctors were wrong. Mina was responding to great changes, seeing Anita like Klara, working in a factory, surviving camps. She was not schizophrenic. No more shock treatment. Just let her be. Albert took good care of her.

But Regina became unwell. I begged her to seek medical care. I made David drive her to St. Joseph's Hospital. She was rushed into surgery. Her appendix had ruptured. Papa's room was below hers. He had Prostrate issues.

My mother-in-law came to watch Anita as I took a taxi to see Regina. Abe was already there, as was David. The doctor was covering Regina with a sheet. She was dead.

I don't remember much after that. Maybe I fainted. When I awoke, David with me. He hugged me. My father-in-law was there, too.

I cried that Regina would have a pauper's funeral, be put into the ground with no stone to mark the spot.

But my father-in -law grabbed my hand.

"No, she won't! I will pay for everything the way it should be!"

And he did. I picked out a beautiful casket for my sister. I bought her a nice dress for her to wear. A rabbi was hired to do the service. A hearse brought Regina to the cemetery. I picked out a nice gravestone to be placed.

From then on, I had great respect for Israel Chernick.

He let me give Regina a place of honor to rest.

I didn't tell Mama Regina was dead. I did tell Papa after he got better and came home.

But Abe told me soon after, with Regina dead, Mina with Albert, me married with a child, our parents had to go to The Jewish Home for the Aged.

I recalled Bubbe had been murdered in Vienna at that Jewish Nursing Home. But I realized that happened under Nazi rule. This was America.

Papa resisted, begged David not to allow it. But my brother was in charge of our parents now. With Anita's needs, no more help from Regina, we couldn't care for Papa, who now had Prostrate Cancer.

So Papa went with Mama. He was allowed to pray in the chapel anytime he wished.

Then a miracle happened. I was pregnant again. Papa was saddened this time. I couldn't understand why at all. Not every baby I had need be like Klara.

I gained weight in this pregnancy. My doctor said all was well. I felt good, strong, and happy. I ignored Papa. He was so negative. There was no reason this time.

I had a healthy baby boy I called Russell, after Regina, and Lloyd after Lazar.

We had the bris. Papa wouldn't come. But Abe did. I was so proud. My little son was normal. He didn't cry much, ate well, let me hold him. My son liked me holding him. Finally, I had a normal child.

David was so pleased. Anita wasn't horrible towards her brother, 8 years younger. I didn't fear she would harm him.

Chapter 13: Cranston

Then I got pregnant again! David decided we needed to move to Cranston, to a bigger house, with no tenants. He said we would live near shops, bus routes, good schools.

Anita became angry. She would not be near Nancy Chin. She had to change schools. And worst of all, she had to stay back a second time. She tested poorly and had to repeat third grade.

I was sorry for Anita, but David decided for the entire family. Russell would be happy here, with his own room. The baby would have a room. Anita would have a big bedroom. David and I had a bigger bedroom. There was a yard. There were Jewish shops. David liked us to keep Kosher. I ate out with my brother, which was fine with my husband.

I had a baby girl. Papa wanted her named for Klara and his niece, my cousin, killed in Treblinka. I let Papa pick those Hebrew names of Klara Esther. Her English name was Cynthia Elise. But David looked at her and always called her Cindy.

Cindy liked being picked up by me. She noticed her environment. And she walked at 9 months old.

She didn't talk at all. But I could tell she understood everything said. Anita tried to hit her. David stopped her and for once, punished her severely.

Russell liked his baby sister. Anita never hit him and he stood protectively by Cindy. Anita did not hurt Russell and would leave Cindy alone when he was around.

Anita did very poorly in school. She began to eat too much and gained weight. I tried to control her eating. Anita would smack my hand hard.

Anita respected David and Abe. So I let them watch her as much as possible.

I concentrated more on Russell and Cindy. Those two children liked me. I sat with them, played with them, fed them. I didn't include Anita during these times. I was peaceful with my two younger children.

I got pregnant again. I took Russell and Cindy to see my parents at the nursing home by bus while David went to work and Anita was at school. Mama held Cindy. Cindy didn't resist. But Mama was now blind.

Papa held Russell, but his hands shook. Russell was very calm. There was no reason for Papa to be nervous. He wasn't confused at all. Russell was well behaved. But I put Russell off of him and placed Cindy there instead.

Papa seemed calmer with Cindy.

"She doesn't speak, Papa.

But Papa said, "She isn't like Klara. She notices everything. She will talk when she is ready."

"But Anita...."

"Papa, Anita is like Klara!"

Papa nodded, "You have one normal child at least!"

"Papa, Cindy and Russell are both normal."

Papa said, "Russell is like Lazar."

"Russell does not have polio!"

Papa looked away, he would not answer me.

Maybe Papa was confused. Russell walked just fine.

I didn't tell Papa I was pregnant again. He would only upset me needlessly.

Papa died a few days later.

We buried him next to Regina. My husband and brother jointly paid for his funeral. It was very respectable.

Mama didn't understand. But she saw me showing with pregnancy.

"Toba", she frowned. She called me by my Hebrew name.

"Yes, Mama?"

"I am so sorry, little bird. Papa and I wanted better for you!"

"But Mama, except for Anita, everything is good. I am gaining weight. It is another healthy pregnancy!"

Mama tried not to cry, "At least one healthy child you have!"

I couldn't understand this at all.

Mama died in late December. We buried her on New Year's Day of 1963, next to Papa and Regina.

My baby born was born the next month. We called him Stuart Scott. After Papa and Mama, Solomon and Schewa.

Cindy could now talk, after Papa said she would. She called the baby, Stuie. We all did, too. Cindy especially loved Stuie from the very start.

Anita seemed not to want to harm this baby boy. Only Cindy did Anita target, besides me of course.

Anita was now 13. She was a terrible student, she was only in 6th grade. But she met a nice boy. He had seizures so he didn't care that Anita was slow.

Anita also made another friend in the neighborhood. Her name was Sharon. She was bright, but had great patience for Anita.
And life went on for us.

Chapter 14: Muscular Dystrophy

Russell went in First Grade. He made so many friends. He was an average student, but he had charisma. He had boys come over to play baseball in our big yard.

But then his teacher called me, said Russell was walking with a gait.
Russell did not have polio so I thought nothing of it. But my brother seemed alarmed. We took Russell to see Dr. Gunita. He told us to take Russell to Boston Children's Hospital.

David was very nervous so we had Anita stay with Sharon that Saturday. We took Cindy and Stuie with us as well as Russell. Cindy would sit with Stuie in the waiting room.

We went in with Russell. Doctors asked me only about my side of the family. I told them about Klara, Regina, and Abe as well as Mina.

They asked if there was any other sibling? I hesitated at first, then said Lazar had polio. They made me give details of his death at Lainz Neuro-Muscular Hospital in Vienna.

They took blood work and urine from Russell. He was very cooperative with them, even cheerful.

But David was not. Something dark was in his mind.

There were questions about Stuie as well. He was only 2. I would allow no testing at all. David left it alone for now.

We drove up a second time to Boston. David was beyond nervous now. Cindy had to tell her father how to go. I said nothing at all.

David and I were ushered into the conference room. Russell was in another room with a social worker

"Russell has Duchenne Muscular Dystrophy, a

genetic, progressive disease passed through the maternal side."

David looked hard at me. He never gave me that look before.

"Did Lazar have it?!"

"NO! He had polio!"

I insisted. It was a mutation. I survived the Holocaust. The doctors looked away from me.

"MY brother, Abe, is fine. He is fine!"

"Yes, but your other brother was not!", David screamed at me.

He calmed down suddenly, but he said, "Your parents had to know the truth!"

"NO!"

David let it go. I was at my breaking point. He loved me enough to stop.

We drove home in silence.

And I was going to treat Russell as I always did. Except, I didn't. I fussed over him. He didn't like it. And soon, David and I began to argue. We never had before. We had a peaceful marriage until then.

Russell's gait worsened. We went to the MDA clinic at Rhode Island Hospital. The doctors there did confront me on family history. I told them I had a lot of knowledge in science. So they talked terms with me I understood.

They suggested that I volunteer for MDAA. I decided I would. The organization gave me funding raising assignments. I networked extensively and raised money easily.

I began to advocate for my son to have a banister installed at school at the entrance of the school yard. It was accomplished. I anticipated he would need a new school to go to next year since climbing stairs became harder for him.

I met with the school board. I dressed well, spoke convincingly, and it was agreed he would be transported to West View, an elementary school on one floor.

I couldn't cook well. Mama had never taught me since I was destined to be a doctor, not a housewife. Daddy hired me a kindly cleaning lady named Katherine. She came twice a week.   Cindy took to her immediately. I was glad. Poor Cindy didn't get much of my time now.

But my brother paid attention to Cindy, so did David.

Cindy never gave me trouble. I was not avoiding her. But Russell began to take most of my time. He required more help. He fell frequently.

I decided to pose a question to his doctors. A heel cord lengthening could help Russell. I gave details why this could work. The doctors agreed with me, but adding it would work for 2 years. No longer.

David agreed Russell could have the surgery. I selected the best orthopedic surgeon in Rhode Island for the job. Blue Cross would only pay so much.

David was making an excellent living now. The Mafia became his best clients. They never jumped bail, they always showed up in court. I spoke Italian to the big bosses who came to our house to pay my husband.

They liked me very much. They only did business with my husband from then.

So Russell had his surgery in Providence. The operation was very successful. Russell would walk for two more years.

Chapter 15: Cindy

Cindy played with Stuie all the time. Stuie was extremely bright. He always did well in school, like I had.

Cindy was a poor student in school, but she easily figured things out. I was proud of her. She was always observing, asking questions.

But one day, Cindy said, "Stuie is getting a gait like Russell. I think he has Muscular Dystrophy."

I am so ashamed at what I did next. I hit Cindy hard across the face!

David was furious at me. Russell rushed to Cindy's side. Anita laughed hard. David demanded Anita stay in her room for a long time.

I easily apologized to my little bird. I knew I was so wrong. Because Cindy was right. Stuie was walking like his big brother had.
I think she forgave me. She didn't act angry towards me. But Anita targeted her more. Cindy didn't take it. She scratched Anita across the arm.

I never punished Cindy. I made the excuse I would cut her nails. I never did. Cindy needed long nails to protect herself against my heavy, older daughter.

David thought he could control Anita. While he was around, he could. But he had work. So during summers, I told David to take Cindy to court with him to teach her about the law. David liked that suggestion. He got it in his head that Cindy would be a lawyer, and never marry, never risk tragedy.

I knew now why Papa wanted me to a doctor, to avoid tragedy.

But I couldn't control myself when I told Cindy that someday medical tests could guide her to know whether she was carrying a girl. I told her her girls would not get this type of Muscular Dystrophy.

David and I always competed to get Cindy to accept our separate feelings on the subject. But I had scientific training David did not have. Cindy respected my educational background and seemed swayed to my thinking.

David pushed education on Cindy. I was fine with the idea Cindy would go to college. I was not okay with David telling her to never to marry.

Cindy began to well in school. She loved history most of all. I had no idea this would divide us.

Cindy never accepted my answers to her questions. I lied to her about my age. She snooped in my room and found my old driver's license with my birth date on it.

Abe would not tell her much. But he did tell how about Vienna before the Holocaust. That he played soccer and chess.

But Cindy asked him whether he was ever in love? He got angry at first. He didn't want to remember that. But she was persistent so he told her about Magda. While visiting Abe one time in his apartment, she found Magda's picture. He was furious at her.

Then, Cindy got beaten up by Anita. Abe saw Cindy black and blue. He was very upset and decided he needed to spend more time with Cindy to keep her away from Anita.

Chapter 16: The Other Shoe Falls

Stuie was finally diagnosed with Muscular Dystrophy as well after a terrible fall at a Muscular Dystrophy event. He seemed to decline faster than Russell did. His decline was more in the spine. I had no procedure I could suggest for that.

Cindy was becoming a good student in fact, but she wasn't eating well. She was losing weight. I let her eat more sweets, I had Abe take her out for dinner. Nothing worked.

I decided Abe and I would to Vienna and take Cindy with us. Let her explore history and maybe save her life.

David agreed immediately. I told him I wanted Cindy to get new clothes for the trip. He said absolutely yes. He would buy her a new camera.

The boys would go to Muscular Dystrophy Camp for two weeks. David would work, but rush to them should anything go wrong.

So we went to London first to see my childhood friend, Elsa. After Cindy rested a long time after jet lag, she began with her questions about Elsa's family. Then she started asking about mine.

I tried not to get upset, but I did. I could tell Cindy would never give up. She would return to England to see Elsa again.

It was on to Vienna. Abe got nervous with Cindy's questions. She insisted on going to the cemetery with us where my grandparents and brother and sister were buried. She was horrified Lazar and Klara had no gravestones. She probed for more answers.

We took her to eat Sacher Torte to avoid answering. But she was not pacified. She at least did eat, our main goal.

We went to Italy. I told her nothing of my time there. It didn't matter. She pumped Benjamin for answers. He gave her a little information, not much.

We returned home where Cindy discussed everything with David. He pledged to her to pay for more trips to Europe.

Chapter 17: Russell

Meanwhile, Russell had become Poster Youth for MDAA. He made appearances for fund raising. I wrote speeches for him, but he delivered them so masterfully. He was so personable. Organization made big donations.

He was invited to meet Jerry Lewis in Las Vegas. Abe had to come babysit Cindy and Stuie for that Labor Day weekend. Russell would appear on the telethon.

David had to go with me to help with Russell. A big Mafia boss sent a limo to take us to the airport.

David never broke the law, was never doing more than bail Mafia members out of jail. But they took such a liking to our family. They saw how our boys stopped walking, how we did everything possible for our children.

Their grandchildren were sent to me to learn Italian. Their wives visited me. Abe took Cindy to their restaurants. They gave Cindy big portions on desserts. In Las Vegas, it was hot. David rented a car and took us to Hoover Dam. We wheeled Russell across into

Arizona and back again. We stayed at a very fancy hotel. The telethon paid for helpers for us at night. Jerry Lewis told me I was an excellent Vice President for the Rhode Island Chapter of MDAA. He gave me his personal card should I have any concerns.
He let me speak to researchers. I wanted to know scientific particulars. They were amazed at my in depth understanding. We spoke about the missing proteins and how to develop something to provide its function.

I was sad in a way I could not complete medical school. More advantage training might have provided me with what I needed to be a researcher. But it was not to be.

Chapter 18: Cindy and Europe

Cindy got to go to Vienna again with Abe and Anita. Anita was nearly 25 now. And Abe would watch her. Cindy was nearly 15 so she could advocate for herself.

But I got an alarmingly call from Abe. Anita apparently picked a fight with a salesclerk and almost committed violence. Cindy had stopped Anita somehow, got her out of the store.

I was relieved, but angry at myself. Anita shouldn't have been allowed to go. Her moods were just too unpredictable.

We would not pay for Anita to go to Europe again. The risk was just too great to take. Anita didn't get much out of it anyhow.

But Cindy was in her element in Europe. She gathered information and then learned even more. Her history teacher told me Cindy knew more about Holocaust than he ever did. She should have received the history award. He admitted she was rob of it.

Cindy entered 10th grade and made a great friend of another history teacher. David Andrew became Cindy's mentor.

My David was so proud of her. He financed all her books and would pay for future trips to Europe. He encouraged her to apply to top schools for college.

But there was a problem. I knew David's aim was for Cindy to get the BA in history so she could go to law school.

I knew my little bird so well. Cindy never wanted to go to law school. She wanted that PHD in European History. But that wouldn't happen either.

Cindy loved history. She was very good in it. But her foreign language skills would never be like mine. She could write well in English, but never would she be fluent in German. She needed German for Holocaust Studies.

So I let things go.

Until Cindy and I went to visit Brandeis. David stayed with the boys while Cindy and I took 5 buses to Waltham. Brandeis was not for my little bird. Cindy had no street smarts. These snobbish people would destroy her self confidence.

I asked David to discourage Cindy about Brandeis. He wouldn't listen to me. Cindy got rejected. Her grades were good, but not her SAT. She was crushed. She had to settle on lesser schools.

But then tragedy shook us terribly.

Chapter 19: Tragedy

I went to get Stuie shoes. They were left downstairs.I came back up to dress Stuie for school. He was dead on his bed. I began to administer CPR while David called for a rescue squad.

The crew kept trying. I knew my son had no pulse, no heart beat, no vitals at all. But David cried so hard that the paramedics took Stuie to the hospital.

I sat in front of the rescue squad. I looked back and saw the flat line. I knew then Stuie was not coming back. The doctors tried at the Hospital, but Stuie was a DOA.

The doctors began to argue with me. They wanted an autopsy done. I called David, told him to get here now!

The fire chief brought David to me. We both argued with the doctors. It was against Jewish law! Muscular Dystrophy killed our son. They were going to over rule us!

David called the Mafia boss who sent his men to chauffeur who we wished to be at the hospital .

Yes, the Mayor of Cranston came, even the police chief, a Senator, a Judge, even MDAA doctors from the clinic.

The doctors backed down. We had our community behind us, Democrat, Republican, Mafia, police, all told how the Chernick did everything for both boys!

Our Jewish undertaker came to take Stuie away quickly because the doctors wavered again.

We wanted a very fast funeral the next day. Because David's friends, the judges, promised no court order would ever be issued to dig Stuie up from his grave.

One of the doctors came to the funeral home to ask questions. The funeral director personally kicked that doctor out.

And that was the end of it. I don't know if David had any more dealings. He would not have told me anyhow.

But David lost part of himself that day.

Poor Cindy took the blunt of David's grief.

Chapter 20: Cindy and Russell

I got obsessed with Russell, keeping him alive. He was in college now. We hired a full-time helper. I taught the helper to look for signs of a head cold.

I volunteered at Roger Williams Hospital, to have strong connections with doctors while Russell was in college during the day.

David stopped talking to Cindy. I don't know why. Cindy had loved Stuie dearly. She was already on the edge. Russell feared more for Cindy than himself.

Then Cindy took a job at Rocky Point Park for the summer before college started. She was to be stuck at a local school. She met S.

David still ignored Cindy, until it was too late. Cindy got engaged so quickly. David snapped out of his grief, to warn Cindy. But Cindy's grief remained unresolved. She married S.

At least David kept her in college by paying the tuition. But we both knew S was no good for her at all.

We had Russell to care for so we had to

leave Cindy to making this mistake.
David and I talked at length how to protect Russell best. We knew a crisis would happen. We had to be prepared to save our son.

Russell had some struggles in college. He was not a gifted student. But Cindy was, although she wasn't reaching her potential right now.

We paid her to help Russell in Sociology. She drove him to meet Narragansett Indians for an assignment. She asked them the questions.

But more importantly, she drove David and Russell to the Girls' Basketball Team games our son announced as a sportscaster. The helper had the weekends off. David stopped driving when Stuie died. But David still was strong. He could lift Russell. We wouldn't allow Cindy to lift. She could get hurt!

Russell had to take a math class in his final semester. I tutored him. I was always good in math. I had to drill him everyday. He needed to get an 80 to pass the course. Russell did it! He got an 88.
He graduated Rhode Island College in 1981.

Cindy came to the ceremony. I saw the black and blue she thought her pant hose hid. I had to pretend not to see it. I was sure David knew long before this.

It was Russell's day. I wanted it to be very happy. So I said nothing to Cindy about what I saw.

I was tempted to ask David's Mafia friends to beat S up.

But I didn't do it. The Nazis beat Jews up in that police station long ago. Cindy should have called the police on him to do everything legally.

She didn't.

Cindy started her senior year of college while Russell took a few courses in Counseling on the graduate level. We again paid Cindy to tutor Russell. She seemed to like the Counseling principles she read and learned about.

But David had her apply to law school. I knew Cindy wouldn't get in anyhow. Her heart wasn't in it. She didn't even like political science at all. I had to let things play out between Cindy and David.

Chapter 21: More Tragedy

Russell came from his courses and began to cough. David ordered a cab to take Russell and me to Roger Williams Hospital's E.R. Russell's doctor met us there.
I told him to order an X-Ray and blood work.
He was almost half my age. He listened to Russell's chest and heartbeat. He then talked down to me.
"Mrs. Chernick, Russell just has a little congestion, that's all!"
"You must do testing. Russell has Muscular Dystrophy!"
"Now, now you did not go to medical school!
I lost my temper, "I learned more in classical high school in Vienna than you ever did in college!"
But Russell got nervous so I had to stop at once.
We went home. David was upset.
"Why isn't he in the hospital?!"
"The doctor wouldn't listen to me!"
We saw Russell get nervous again so we

stopped arguing. I would take Russell to the MDAA clinic tomorrow.

But tomorrow never came.

That night, Russell began choking on his mucus in his throat. This time, David began CPR while I called the rescue squad. David got tired so I resumed CPR on Russell.

As Russell was loaded up to go, I yelled, "Give him an Epi-pen!"

They drove away. A neighbor rushed us to the hospital.

But the doctors told us, "We had lost contact with the paramedics. We couldn't order the Epi-Pen!"

"I told them to give it to Russell!"

"Mrs. Chernick, it wouldn't have legal without our permission!"

Russell had to have a breathing tube inserted to live. David and I hesitated for a minute, but our emotions ran us. We agreed.

I called Cindy to come to the hospital, but not Anita. We would tell her, but not tonight.

Cindy was informed by the doctors about her brother's condition. We didn't have the energy left to tell her.

We all left that night.

Cindy returned on her own the next day. Then Anita arrived. There was no fighting at all. Anita totally did not bother Cindy, except to ask her opinion.

And then my brother came to the hospital. Cindy cornered him, "This is the

same as what happened to Uncle Lazar?!"
 Abe didn't answer, he didn't have to.
 We all looked at Russell. When his eyes
opened, they had a glass like appearance. I
knew his brain stem was the last to go.
 Cindy spoke to her father and me, "Please,
Russell wants you both to let go!"
 We nodded. We knew that, we resisted it, but
now we had to do the unthinkable
 David and I both had to sign the papers to
take Russell off all life support.
 The next day, Russell died at Rhode Island
Hospital, in ICU. No doctor asked for an
autopsy.
But I called the other physician.
  "Russell is dead!"
  "He isn't here!"
  "He went to Rhode Island Hospital by rescue
squad. "
The doctor screamed in fear, "Please don't sue
me!"
  "You come to his funeral. Don't talk to us.
But I want you to see what you did to my
son!
If you don't come, we will sue you!"
 I saw Cindy the day before the funeral.
 Something terrible happened to her. I told
David to go talk to S.
      I heard what he said, "My wife is taking
Cindy shopping for funeral clothes. You are
not to interfere. If you do, I have friends who
will come see you instead!"
 S. Got very white in the face. He understood

perfectly.

I took Cindy shopping. David said I was to buy her a new dress, shoes, a purse, pant hose, and to spend alot of money on her.

And I did. I don't know how I managed, but Russell was dead, and Cindy was alive.

The funeral was dignified. David and I asked Michael Nordstrom to give the eulogy. He was Russell's friend and advocate at RIC. Rabbi Franklin conducted the funeral service in both Hebrew and English.

Then we put Russell in the ground next to Stuie. Our boys were together again.

Chapter 22: Cancer

We had Cindy and Anita left.
But David had blood in his urine. I made him
go to the doctor and told the doctor David
needed to be tested for Bladder Cancer.
I was sorry I was right.

But in the meantime, I told my political
friends to get a bill passed in which
paramedics can use their own discretion in
case communications are lost with the
hospital.
I got to testify before a committee. I spoke
very well, presenting medical facts and my
personal account of what happened to Russell.

The bills almost died because private ambulances were
afraid to be sued. I offered a compromise to let them be
exempt and only have public paramedics use their judgment.
The bill passed.

But now David had Cancer.
I heard about a trial being held at Roger Williams Hospital for
my husband's particular strain. I used my influence to get him
admitted to the experimental program.

David only did it to buy him some time. He wanted
to prepare me for his death. He would transfer the house deed
in my name only. He taught me the finances. Then, he needed

to vacate his bail bondsmen cases still pending.

Cindy would have to drive me around the state to courthouses to do it. Mostly, judges were courteous towards me. Lawyers were polite. Sheriffs were very kind. Defendants were the nicest of all.

But one judge was rude to me. I was trying to remain professional. It was the defendant who spoke up. No sheriff even tried to silence him.

"Excuse me, your honor, but Mrs. Chernick is acting on behalf of her dying husband. He wants to transfer cases to make it easier on the court system.

You are being very rude to her.
You need to apologize!"

The judge saw no sheriff protesting at all.
In fact, a sheriff said, "Your Honor, Mrs. Chernick is waiting patiently for your ruling!"

The judge nearly whispered, "Okay, the motion to transfer this case to another bondsman is granted. Mrs. Chernick will receive the refund on bail."

Yes, you guessed it, that client was a member of the Mafia.
He shook my hand, "Mrs. Chernick, please let us know if there anything we can do for Mr. Chernick or you!"

Cindy and I drove to the hospital to see David.
"Tina, I want to go home to die".
I peeked at his chart by his bed and saw all the lab values.
"Okay, David, you come home now!"
It was suppose to be three months, it was three days.

On the second day, when Cindy was with me, I called the rescue squad. Cindy argued with me, pleaded with me.

I had no time to explain why.
I ordered the paramedics to administer morphine. My husband

had such terrible pain. They did what I said.
And they did not take him to the hospital. I never intended that.

Cindy understood now what I was trying to accomplish and was okay with what I did.

Anita showed up, so did my brother, and David's siblings. Our Italian neighbor walked up the stairs to see David in bed. My political friend came and members of the Mafia and their wives. Everyone cooked, cleaned, and chatted.

My friend, Edith, whose family was rich in Vienna, came to stay with David, to take his vital signs. I could have done it, but Edith told me I was too close to the case.

Edith came downstairs and said the doctor needed to pronounce David dead. Our doctor arrived and confirmed that my husband was gone.

Chapter 23: Cindy's Grief

Cindy raced out of the house then. Even Anita was worried where she went in the darkness. Cindy's husband tried to run after her. Anita took hold of his arm, "You leave my sister alone!"

Anita had hit her sister plenty of times, but somehow, it wasn't acceptable that the husband did it, too.

Cindy returned an hour later. Her father's body had been removed by the undertaker. She went home with her husband. Anita added for good measure, "You should have let me beat him up!"

I nodded, "Well, your sister has to decide to get rid of him!"

I never admitted that I had the Mafia to do that, but didn't choose to do it. I still wanted Cindy to see what she needed to do.

Cindy had been accepted to a Master's Level Counseling Program. She did well in it. But that husband of hers got a job in Florida. Cindy went with him.

I feared for her life, but until she decided to leave him, there was nothing I could do.

Cindy called me to say she was pregnant. She was frightened of course. I made some calls and found out there was a test to determine the sex of the fetus. I booked an appointment in Philadelphia. I would fly out to meet Cindy there and pay for her flight from Florida.

But a short time later, Cindy called again. She had been beaten yesterday. Her husband was at work. She asked me finally to rescue her.

I told her to drive to the Orlando Airport at once. I called the chief of police I knew well in Rhode Island. He contacted airport security in Florida. Cindy would be protected once she reached the airport.

I called the airline next. All I could book was a flight to Boston. I had to find a way to retrieve her in Boston. My Mafia friends would have sent a limo and bodyguard for her at Logan.

But there was no need. Cindy's flight made an emergency landing in Providence. I was notified by Cindy. I called her best friend to pick her up and take her to the Hospital. It was my idea for the doctors to take pictures of Cindy's many bruises.

Cindy came home to me, but not in a box, as I feared.

Chapter 24: Tests

We still had that appointment in Philadelphia. But we flew together from Rhode Island.

My brother-in-law and sister-in-law hosted us. She in fact drove us to the hospital for the invasive test.

Cindy got upset. But we had to get her through it somehow. The doctors made sure Cindy wasn't bleeding after the test. She wasn't.

So we flew home to wait a week for the results.

Chapter 25: Difficult Pregnancy and Birth

Cindy came running out to the yard screaming, "It's a girl. Her name is Robin!"

But all was not well. Cindy got Pre-Eclampsia. She had to lay down to get the blood pressure down. Her best friend visited, even Anita came.

"Mom, Cindy's legs are so swollen!"

I nodded. It was true.

Then came the morning when Cindy was covered in blood. The carpet looked like the Red Sea. I called the rescue squad, but Cindy kept running around the apartment screaming!

I got our neighbor to come in make Cindy stop moving.

The rescue squad came. I rode in front.

When she got there, the older doctor was waiting.

I didn't mean to be rude, but I had to say it, "Please! Get Dr. Di Zoglio here. Only he can save them both!"

The doctor listened to me. Dr. Di Zoglio arrived to scrub in for emergency surgery.

"Her placenta separated!", I told him, "She may not live through General Anesthesia!"

He nodded, "Yes, we will do a local!"

And he listened to me. He not only saved Cindy, but Robin lived, too.

She was 5 weeks premature and went into the NICU. I was torn whether to be with my daughter or granddaughter.

Cindy said, "Be with Robin!"

So I do as she said.

I was impressed by the staff in NICU. They knew their business. I didn't need to make any comments at all.

Cindy's best friend arrived. I ordered she be allowed to see Robin. Then she rushed to see Cindy.

If that wasn't enough, Cindy's in-laws came. They insulted the baby and made Cindy cry! I had a word with them, "Do I have to have you thrown out? They took me seriously and left on their own accord. They promised to behave better in the future.

We had the baby naming a few months later. I paid

my neighbor to make a special cake Cindy would like.

Chapter 26: The Fall Out

But I just couldn't get Cindy to cooperate with me much after the baby came home. I had medical knowledge Cindy lacked. I only wanted what was best for both Robin and Cindy.

Cindy did work to finish her Master's Degree in Counseling. I babysat so she could attend classes and study. But she wasn't eating well again. The more we argued, the thinner my younger daughter got.

My brother got sick, too. He was in and out nursing homes. I did try to help, but I was preoccupied with Cindy and Robin.

I convinced Cindy to see a doctor friend of mine. Maybe he could get her to see that she needed my help for now? But when he called me on the phone, I was shocked by what he said.

"Tina, you have to let go.

Cindy needs to make her own decisions about her life and the baby."

"She is getting divorced, she has no job, no place to live. I can provide for them."

"Are you listening to yourself? You mean well, but you want to control her!"

"She made bad mistakes!"

"Yes, and she will make more mistakes. But it is her life to live. Robin is her baby, not yours.
Help her, if she asks for it.
Let her go, Tina, or she will starve to death. The not eating is a symptom, not the problem.
Right now, you are the problem."

I was heartbroken, but I trusted this man. I had to accept his advice.

Before Cindy got her Master's Degree in May, my brother, Abe, passed away in April. He made me promise to use his money to buy her a washing machine for Cindy's new small apartment.
But he had no money left.

I told Cindy there would be no washing machine. She argued with me, saying Uncle Abe wanted her to have it. I didn't have to, but I did buy the washing machine for her.

So she and Robin moved out to a dumpy neighborhood on Hartford Avenue. Cindy had the degree, but no job yet. Her best friend lived upstairs from her. There at least was someone to help in an emergency.

And believe it or not, Anita bought Cindy some housewarming items.

Cindy also had a new boyfriend. I admit it, he was handsome, but not a family kind of guy. It would never last. But I stayed out of her business.

Then Cindy did get a job as a Career Counselor. She asked whether I would give her money to buy professional attire? I gave it to her.

Cindy dumped her boyfriend. I was both sad and glad at the same time. She got another one. He was only half-

Jewish, but very polite. He had good manners. I think Cindy liked his British accent. But he was good with Robin.

But Cindy's boss made her unhappy. The boss just micro-managed her. I knew from experience that wouldn't work well. She quit! She didn't have another job yet. I did lecture her, then gave her money to buy food.

She got another job, a better one, as a Director of Social Work in a nursing home. She did good work there working with younger patients. That made sense to me since she grew up with two physically disabled brothers.

Chapter 27: A New Marriage

So Cindy wanted to get remarried. His name was David, like her Daddy. He hesitated, but then agreed.

His Mom flew out from England. She was a lovely woman! She was educated, kindly, great with Robin. We hit it off immediately.

I told Anita not to come to this wedding. She had been good for awhile with Cindy, but got jealous when her younger sister got engaged. She actually hit her sister again.

I decided to move to Providence. The apartment in Warwick was too far away. Cindy was remarried. She wasn't ever going to move back with me.

My sister-in-law had a nice apartment on the East Side for Cindy, David, and Robin to live. It was close to Cindy's work and Robin's school, and closer to me as well.

I admit it. I snooped there while they were at work and school. I wanted to make sure they weren't behind on any bills. They weren't.

Then I met a man at the Hamilton House. His name was Frank Jordan. He wasn't Jewish, but a very smart man. He spoke many languages, like me. He understood science. I was probably a little better in Chemistry than he was, but he knew nature. He didn't hit it off with Cindy, but he liked Robin.

So I married him. We wanted a yard so I bought a small house in Garden City. He taught Robin how to bake. He liked bird watching. But I wouldn't let bees be in my backyard for honey making.

Chapter 28: Yet Another Tragedy

But then, I got the call. My daughter, Anita, was found on her apartment floor. Frank rushed me to the hospital. Apparently, Anita had a massive stroke. She was on the floor for 10 hours!

I had to call Cindy to tell her because Anita was not responding to treatment.
I told Cindy not to go down there yet, but she did anyhow. She told me to get back to the hospital

immediately.

I knew what would be said. The next day was Thanksgiving. I asked to give my answer on Friday.

Cindy and Frank were not to discuss it with me on Thanksgiving. We were to eat the meal with Robin and Cindy's husband at the Hamilton House peacefully. They did as I told them to do.

On Friday, I gave my answer to unplug Anita from all life support. Cindy, Frank, and I were there when my eldest child died. There was nothing to say. Anita became brain dead. She hated sitting around with nothing to do, nowhere to go. I couldn't let her have this living death.

At the funeral, her factory coworkers started to yell at me. Anita had told lies about me. Cindy yelled back that I had paid all major bills, that Anita could be violent at times. They were stunned. My sister-in-law agreed that I had helped Anita financially. So they backed off.

It was not the dignified funeral I had wanted for Anita. But nothing could be done about it.

We went back home to serve guests for the Shiva. No factory workers came, just my friends, Cindy's friends, and Frank's relatives. It was peaceful again.

Frank and I went to clean out her apartment. We found hidden candy and enough cosmetics to fill a department store. There was Twinkie Puffs the Cat. Cindy found a good home for her with the groomer Anita had used.

Chapter 29: More Troubles

Cindy was quite sick with Asthma by this time. I worried about her. Her husband was now mentally ill, and he smoked from pipes.

Robin had been in private schools I paid for. But the latest school wasn't working out.   Cindy was my final, surviving child. I needed to do something to help her. I bought her a house in Warwick. Robin had a good public school to attend and made new friends. Cindy couldn't work full time anymore. So she worked part-time. She worked at the polls, in a clock shop, and finally as a special needs teacher's assistant. She was a substitute so she worked in many schools. She was very good at this job, and she was writing freelance for newspapers.

But she just got too sick to work anymore. Robin kept calling me, saying her Mom was rushed to the hospital. Frank wondered whether Cindy would die and we would have Robin to raise for a few years.

Then, my memory wasn't so good anymore. I lost track of Cindy being in the hospital or not. And I stopped helping Cindy, too. I wasn't mad at her, I just assumed she could manage.

Robin wanted to visit Savannah to see of she wanted to go to college there. Cindy's father-in-law in England died and left them money. And now Cindy was on disability, so was her husband .

The school was expensive. But I agreed to pay for her to go. Cindy had to do the legwork, all the paperwork, I just wrote the check.

Robin stayed 7 weeks in Savannah then begged to come home. She had a boyfriend in Massachusetts. So Cindy went to get her. But Robin moved to Massachusetts to go to school and be with her boyfriend.

Robin returned to Rhode Island with her boyfriend in tow. They lived with Cindy and David. And then Robin got pregnant.

Chapter 30: A New Generation

I had to pay for two expensive tests. Because it was a boy, but the second test showed he would not have Muscular Dystrophy.

Scott, my great-grandson, was born. I was delighted. Even Frank was, too. Scott had beautiful, blue eyes and light hair. Cindy talked the parents into the name. It was Stuie's middle name.

Robin's boyfriend's parents were good people. They hosted the bris in their lovely home. They treated me with great respect.

Then, Cindy announced she had to sell her house. She said they couldn't pay the taxes on it. Her husband then was told to leave. Cindy was divorcing him.

Everything happened so fast, I couldn't keep track anymore. Robin got married. Cindy paid for it because she sold the house. She was still friends with David.

I sold my house, too. Frank said we couldn't manage it. He was too frail, he said I was confused! So we went to West Bay Manor. Frank and I had a hard time adjusting to it. It wasn't our home. But we made do. Scott came to see us with Cindy sometimes. What a delight he was.

Cindy and Robin weren't getting along so she

moved into her own apartment. Then, Cindy received her divorce and got a new boyfriend.

He was handsome! But he lived on Long Island!

I decided to buy Robin a house to live in with Scott and her husband. I thought that was a good idea.

Chapter 31: Everyone Is Moving!

But Robin moved away to Florida with her family the following year. Poor Cindy! It was hard on her.

Cindy stayed in Rhode Island 7 more months, keeping an eye on Frank and me. But then her apartment was in a flood zone. Her boyfriend invited her to live on Long Island.

But she came back every week, staying the whole day, then leaving again. Even Frank was amazed at all the driving she did just to see us!

Then Frank got very sick. He was dying! I needed Cindy to stay with him in Hospice since I couldn't. I paid for her hotel for a week. She sat all day with Frank. Frank's daughter arrived to say good-bye to her father.

Frank died in April of 2011. Cindy sat next to me for the funeral. She coughed a lot. She took me in and out of the car for the reception afterwards.

Cindy decided to move me into Tamarisk. She said the care was better there. So I stayed. Cindy came often to see me, but I got very confused. She sometimes brought Scott, too. He was visiting from Florida.

Chapter 32: Arrangements

Cindy had the undertaker come see me to pre-pay my funeral and burial. I wrote the check, but Cindy to make all the decisions about it. I showed Cindy my DNR papers and instructions. She was to follow what I wanted, which was no heroics at all.

Cindy signed for Hospice to come. I had 6 months to live. I knew that Tamarisk was very expensive and I went through my money. There would be no money for Cindy to inherit.

But, I hoped this guy she was with would take care of her.

I got very tired easily. I saw my mother who beckoned me to come to her.

But I asked Cindy first, "Would you be okay?"

I know Cindy lied when she said, "Yes!"

Yet, I decided it was time.

Cindy was called and rushed in from Long Island. She sat with me all day, but I was so nervous. My tooth fell out. I had bad pain. So my doctor gave me something to relax me. I went into a coma.

But I heard Cindy tell me heaven was beautiful, that

everyone was waiting for me.
So I left her behind.

Chapter 33: Cindy's Relationship With Me Now

It has been 4 plus years now.
Cindy left her boyfriend recently and moved to Florida.

But she is very poor now. So she started writing two books, one about her life, this one about mine.

I hope she makes money doing this. She is quite good at writing. Even Frank thought so.

I was generous to her financially, most of the time. I got confused and made bad decisions. I let Cindy put me into an expensive place. She wanted the best for me, as I always wanted for her and Robin.

My granddaughter, Robin, had been very sick. She had Cervix Cancer. Cindy prayed for me to save Robin. And Robin did survive.

And now, Cindy prays to me again, to help sell these books. But Scott, my great-grandson, can help her with that.
But, I think she will make money.

Well, here in heaven, we can only slip in and out of the lives of our loved ones we left behind.
Cindy's brothers, her Dad, her Uncle Abe, her dear mother-in-law, her friend, Aron, Katherine, even Anita, and me, are all cheering for her to succeed with her writing.
Hopefully, what she wrote about me will sell.

I taught her what I could, but as my doctor friend once told me, "Cindy will make mistakes. But it is her life to live".

Chapter 34: My Final Words For Cindy

Dear little bird,

It is up to you now. I will always put a good word in on your behalf, but you have to follow through. Keep trying! Don't give up.

Remember, walk with one foot in front of the other!

Love,

Your Mom in heaven